D0425554

THE WAY OF THE MYSTICS

The Way of the Mystics

By

H. C. GRAEF

THE MERCIER PRESS, LTD.,
CORK

63957

FIRST PUBLISHED 1948

Nihil Obstat : JACOBUS P. BASTIBLE,
Censor Deputatus.

Imprimatur : ✠ DANIEL,
Episcopus Corcagiensis.

1 *Octobris,* 1947.

BV
5095
A1
G7

PRINTED IN EIRE
BY CAHILL AND CO., LTD.
PARKGATE PRINTING WORKS
DUBLIN

World copyright reserved. The Mercier Press Ltd., Cork

PREFACE

THE substance of a number of the following studies has appeared in *Blackfriars* and *The Life of the Spirit*, to the Editor of which I wish to make the customary acknowledgments, at the same time thanking him for his unfailing encouragement. The essay on St. Hildegard was first published in the *Dublin Review*. The translations used are taken from the works cited in the bibliography or are my own.

REGINAE SACRATISSIMI ROSARII

CONTENTS

INTRODUCTION

THE THEOLOGICAL FOUNDATIONS OF MYSTICISM

THERE is in our time, as in most periods of unrest and insecurity, a great and widespread interest in mysticism, and as a kind of corollary, also a pronounced defiance of it. There are those who seek it as a welcome means of escape from the hard realities with which humanity is faced ; and there are others who condemn it for this same reason, because they see in it an obstacle to their dream of building a " brave new world." The paradoxical fact is that both are superficially right, and yet are fundamentally wrong. It is true that for the mystic this world of " stark realities " is not the ultimate Reality (as it is for no believing Christian), but this is precisely why mysticism does not attempt to escape from reality. On the contrary, by overcoming earthly reality, the mystic seeks to attain to heavenly Reality. Now the heavenly Reality can never be reached without suffering from the earthly realities. But the " realist "—in the popular, not in the philosophical sense of the term—strives for the realisation of his new world without suffering, with neither poverty nor disease, nor any of those other disturbing weaknesses that flesh is heir to. He seeks a life regulated by science so as to eliminate pain ; he dreams of great freedoms, especially freedom from any kind of fear— though as far as the memory of mankind reaches back there has never been a time when man has lived entirely free from fear, except for a small band who followed closely in the footsteps of Him who said : " Fear not those who kill the body. . . ." It is not the politicians who will free mankind from fear—how should they, as they can abolish neither death nor disease, least of all their cause, which is sin ?

The mystic does not indulge in such idle dreams, for he knows a more excellent way : Love alone, which is stronger than death, can cast out fear, and the annals of sanctity are the records of its victories. It is not the mystics who run away from reality. Because they have found Reality, that which men usually call by this name presents no more difficulties for them. And this is the proof

that theirs is not a pleasant form of escape, but an overcoming
of all fear of "reality" by a greater power, by the power of
Charity. The mystic, the lover *par excellence*, is the only true
Realist, in that he is the master of "reality," whereas most of
his fellowmen are mastered by it. Therefore the attraction of
the "escapists" for mysticism is as unfounded as the fear of the
"realists," for it is far above the level of either.

There is another kind of interest, and another kind of fear.
There are the pious, eager for supernatural experiences, who
ardently wish to have revelations like St. Catherine of Siena and
visions and locutions like St. Teresa. And there are those who
cry "illusion" the moment a soul desires to give up point by
point meditation. Here again, both are wrong. For visions and
revelations, indeed, are not to be desired, but neither is discursive
meditation, except as a preparation for more perfect prayer.
But here we are already in the thick of theological controversies,
and only the highest theological principles can give us the right
solution of the problem.

St. Thomas Aquinas did not write a special treatise on mystic
theology. In the golden age of Scholasticism there were no hard
and fast divisions between systematic, moral, ascetical and mystical
theology ; but systematic theology furnished the rules by which
to deal with the practical questions of the spiritual life. And so
the Angelic Doctor gives us the principles of mystical theology,
embedded in the *Prima Secundae* of his *Summa Theologica*, which
deals with man, made in the image of God, and with his virtues
and vices in general (especially question 68, on the Gifts of the
Holy Ghost) and in the *Secunda Secundae*, which treats of particular
virtues and states of life (especially questions 180 to 182, on the
Contemplative and Active Life) and in his whole teaching on Grace
and the virtues.

The mystical life is nothing else but the life of grace lived at its
highest level. For there is only one principle of the supernatural
life, sanctifying grace, which is, as it were, the beginning of eternal
life here below (*quaedam inchoatio vitae aeternae*), and it is by this
principle that all souls must live, whether they be newly baptized
infants, converted sinners, or Saints practising the virtues in a heroic
degree. For just as the whole plant is contained in the tiny seed,
so that no external addition is needed to produce leaves, flowers
and fruits in their season, so in the supernatural "seed" of grace

there is already present in germ the whole organism of the mystic life which needs, therefore, no other principle to explain it. For the life of grace unfolds itself principally in the virtues, more particularly in the theological virtues of faith, hope and charity, and in the Seven Gifts of the Holy Ghost, enumerated in Isaiah (11, 2). Both, as St. Thomas proves (*Prima Secundae*, q. 68 a.2), are necessary for salvation, for without the Gifts the life of grace would be incomplete. The reason for this is that, practising the theological virtues, man still acts in a human manner, for, with our reason and will, though informed by faith, hope and charity, we can know and love God only imperfectly ; in order to become capable of our supernatural end we must be moved in a supernatural manner, and this is done by the motion of the Holy Ghost.

Yet, the infusion of the Gifts at Baptism or at the return to the state of grace in conversion does not mean that we are immediately guided in this superhuman manner. In fact, in the beginning of the spiritual life, that is to say in the purgative way, the Gifts are still, so to speak, in an embryonic state. They are there, but they are hardly noticeable—just as there is no trace of a flower before the bud becomes visible, though the plant already contains all that is necessary to produce it. In the purgative state there are still far too many obstacles in the way of the Holy Ghost ; as long as self-love is yet strong, uncreated Love cannot take over the government of the soul. This, therefore, is the time when she has to do most of the work herself—always aided by grace, that goes without saying. She meditates to incite in herself hatred of sin and love of virtue, she reflects and weighs her motives before she acts, she performs penances, and generally employs all the means recommended by the Church and by her spiritual guide to wean herself from the ill-regulated love of creatures. Her whole spiritual life is very active, dominated by reason and will under the influence of grace.

But, as St. Thomas says, the active life prepares for the contemplative life, as the imperfect leads to the perfect, " for the contemplative life is directed to the love of God, not of any degree, but to that which is perfect " (*Secunda Secundae*, q. 182, a.4, ad 1um). Therefore, if we would be perfect, we must be contemplatives. Not, indeed, members of Contemplative Orders, but our spiritual life, whatever our " state," whether active, contemplative or mixed, must have the signs of contemplation.

Now contemplation develops under the progressively increasing influence of the Gifts of the Holy Ghost, especially the gifts of understanding and of wisdom. As it is brought about by the action of the Holy Ghost and not by our human activity it cannot be reached by our own efforts, but we can prepare for it by prayer, penance and good works, or, in other words, by faithfully following the purgative way. Then, in the normal course of the spiritual life, a day will come when the Holy Ghost will begin to take the lead and to introduce the soul into the " passive " ways, beginning with the " Night of the Senses," so vividly described by St. John of the Cross in the *Ascent of Mount Carmel*. This " Night " is very painful because the soul suddenly finds herself deprived of her own activities in which she found pleasure. Now she kneels down to pray and not a thought, not an image presents itself—for the work of man has now to give place to the work of God, the Gifts begin to perfect the faculties of the soul to make them pliable to the action of the Holy Ghost (cf. *Prima Secundae*, q. 68 a.8). This is the beginning of the Illuminative Way, to which corresponds St. Teresa's Prayer of Recollection and especially the Prayer of Quiet, i.e., the first forms of contemplative prayer properly so called.

Now Contemplation is a term often very vaguely used, almost as vaguely as mysticism. According to St. Thomas, who follows Pseudo-Dionysius, it is essentially an operation of the intellect, in its perfection represented by the circular movement. The human mind, after being purified (by penance and meditation) from its two defects of clinging to external things and of discursive reasoning, abandons the latter and is introduced to the " simple contemplation of intelligible truth " (*Secunda Secundae*, q. 180, a.6). In this operation there can be no error, because it has to do with first principles, which are known by simple intuition (*simplici intuitu*), so that the soul becomes like the angels, having abandoned all else and resting in the sole contemplation of God, as far as is possible for an embodied spirit, whose contemplation, it must be borne in mind, can never be entirely freed from all imagery. This simple contemplation, however, is not a joyless intellectual exercise, on the contrary, it is the one perfectly satisfying human activity, because it pertains to the essence of man as *animal rationale*, whose very nature demands the contemplation of Truth (*Secunda Secundae*, q. 180, a.7), and is, therefore, accompanied by delectation. Now if this is so on the natural plane, how much more on the supernatural, when the soul is moved to the contemplation of God by charity. For "this is the ultimate perfection of the contemplative life, namely, that the Divine Truth be not only seen but also loved" (ibid., ad I^{um}). In this it differs profoundly from the contemplation of the pagan philosophers and all other "natural contemplation," which lacks this ultimate perfection, because the soul of the unbeliever is not joined to the object of her contemplation by charity, the *vinculum perfectionis*.

For as contemplative prayer progresses, charity grows and the work of the Gifts becomes more apparent. The soul, though, of course, always under obedience to her director, tends more and more to act under inspiration instead of following her own devices, just as the form and contents of her prayer no longer depend on her choice. Yet at this stage the supernatural plant has brought forth only flowers, it has not yet yielded its fruits. The soul is still full of imperfections, which are seen the more clearly the more she progresses in contemplation. As St. Thomas says, "when man attains to the contemplation of truth he loves it yet ardently, while he hates the more his own deficiency and the weight of his corruptible body" (*Secunda Secundae*, q. 180, a. 7 ad I^{um}). St. John of the Cross gives a terrifying list of these imperfections, corresponding to the Seven Deadly Sins. In order to rid the soul of these last obstacles to the full action of the Gifts she is now introduced into the "Night of the Spirit"—a series of most painful purifications which may continue for a long time, even while the soul already enjoys full union and ecstasy, that is, when she has emerged from the illuminative into the unitive way. It is only after these last purgings that she is brought fully under the domination of the Gifts. In the "transforming Union," the immediate prelude to the Beatific Vision, her almost uninterrupted union with God enables her to judge all things by the wisdom of the Holy Ghost. With her own reason and will in complete subjection to the Divine action, she can truly say that she lives, no longer herself, but that Christ lives in her. The seed sown by the Divine Sower has brought forth its fruit and will soon be ready to be gathered into the barn, and the soul will at last hear the long-desired words : *Euge, serve bone et fidelis . . . intra in gaudium Domini tui.*

The mystic state, surrounded with so much splendour in the lives of the Saints—is it really nothing but this "normal" develop-

ment of the virtues and the gifts? Why, then, do the mystics,
a St. Bernard, a St. Catherine of Siena, a St. John of the Cross,
seem so different from ourselves? How can the mystical life,
which in them abounds in visions, locutions, stigmata and other
marvellous experiences, rest on the same principles as our own,
devoid of all these things? It would seem to be this consideration
that has led many modern theologians and spiritual writers to
assume that the mystic state is "extraordinary" in the strict
sense, i.e., that it is not in the normal way of sanctity. In fact
attempts have been made to divide the spiritual life into two
completely separate compartments: the one ascetical and
"normal," with an ascetical purgative, illuminative and unitive
way, the other mystic and "extraordinary," with the same three
ways. There is no necessity to repeat the arguments against this
view so convincingly stated by theologians like Saudreau and
Garrigou-Lagrange. We would only say that, if this modern
theory were true, the unity of the spiritual life, built on the virtues
and the Gifts, would be broken up, and the traditional teaching
of St. Thomas, St. John of the Cross, and all the older theologians
and mystics would have to be at least re-interpreted in a manner
entirely different from its commonly accepted meaning.

What is the reason for this change of outlook? If we consider
the works of two of the chief modern representatives of the two
schools, the Jesuit Père Poulain, and the Dominican Père Garrigou-
Lagrange, their different approach to the subject of mysticism
is at once obvious. Poulain describes mystic phenomena, Garrigou-
Lagrange establishes the theological foundations on which Christian
mysticism rests. In other words, the one treats the subject as a
scientist, the other as a metaphysician. Now the scientist has to
deal with phenomena, he investigates things that can be observed.
But the working of grace is invisible, neither the virtues nor the
Gifts of the Holy Ghost can be seen, heard or handled—therefore
the man with the scientific bent of mind will find little to attract
him in these theological conceptions. It is different with the
extraordinary phenomena frequently accompanying the mystic
state. They afford ample material for the scientist. Even in the
lower strata of the mystic life, in the Prayer of Quiet, there is already
the "ligature" of the senses, for example the partial inability
to move, which becomes more marked in the Prayer of Union.
Then there are visions and locutions, and in ecstasy such striking

phenomena as levitation, bilocation, the gift of tears and many other conspicuous graces. But, strangely enough, what attracts the scientist and makes him consider the mystic state as "extraordinary" in the strict sense, is of comparatively small interest to the theologian. In this respect the latter is a faithful disciple of St. Paul, who reprimanded the Corinthians for being too fond of these exciting gifts and taught them to prefer the edifying ones, and, above all, Charity, the queen of virtues.

The reason for the depreciation of extraordinary phenomena on the part of the theologians is that they are not *gratiae gratum facientes*, but *gratiae gratis datae*, i.e., they are not required for the sanctification of the soul, but given for other purposes, such as the demonstration of the sanctity of their recipient to others, or the conversion of sinners or heretics. Moreover, as they are not supernatural *quoad essentiam* (essentially) but only *quoad modum* (in the way they work) these phenomena may be imitated by the devil, or they may even proceed from nothing higher than a vivid imagination or a hysterical temperament, in which latter case they are, of course, neither supernatural nor preternatural. For this reason the theologians though taking account of them, are comparatively little concerned with these external manifestations, and if they investigate them, as St. Thomas does in his treatises on prophecy (*Secunda Secundae* qq. 171–74), rapture (ibid. 175) and other *gratiae gratis datae*, they do not give descriptions of the phenomena but reduce them to their theological principles, analysing their essence, cause, relations to the cognitive and appetitive faculties and similar points of metaphysical interest. But, being *gratiae gratis datae*, they do not constitute the essence of mysticism, though some of them frequently accompany it, especially in its higher stages.

There is one more objection made by those who hold that mysticism is something essentially extraordinary, superadded to the ordinary life of grace, and that is the fact that there are so few mystics. We have said that out of the insignificant seed there develop magnificent trees and flowers, and we applied this simile to the spiritual life. But, if this metaphor holds good, why does not grace bring forth mystics as frequently as acorns produce oaks (to use one of the favourite metaphors of Garrigou-Lagrange)? Now, even in the natural sphere seeds do not produce plants and plants do not produce fruits unless placed in congenial soil and given the amount of rain and sunshine they need. Thus unfavourable surroundings or unsuitable direction can go far to prevent the normal development of the germ of grace implanted in the soul at Baptism. Our Lord Himself used the parable of the Sower and his good seed, of which yet only the fourth part bore fruit, and even that fourth part not all a hundredfold ! The obstacles He mentions in the parable, the interference of Satan, tribulations and persecutions, the cares and allurements of the world, they all enter into the spiritual life, preventing the full development of grace. For man is endowed with free-will. This is the very capacity that makes him fit for the moral and spiritual life, but, and this is the other side of the picture, it can also refuse co-operation with grace, or can co-operate only in a half-hearted manner. Now the mystic life, which is beset with sufferings and temptations, needs the full co-operation of the will, which becomes especially difficult in the two " Nights " of the Senses and of the Spirit, the two great crises of the life of contemplation, which mark the transition from the state of beginners to that of proficients and again to that of the perfect. It is especially during these testing times that souls may fall away by their own fault, so that the mystic life is either prevented altogether, or stunted in its growth. It is, therefore, not surprising, that given all these obstacles of unsuitable surroundings, lack of direction, a particularly " active " and restless temperament, insufficient generosity, and many others besides, the full mystic life should be very rare here below and appear as something extraordinary, though it is meant to be the normal crown of the Christian life.

And how could it be otherwise, as the supernatural end for which we were created is the contemplation of God in the Beatific Vision and sanctifying grace its beginning here on earth ? There is, therefore, almost as much reason to desire the mystical life as there is to desire the Beatific Vision. Its two great effects are a thorough purification from our sins and imperfections, and a corresponding growth in union with God—surely the two things most to be desired by every fervent Christian. Père Poulain himself has proved in his *The Graces of Interior Prayer* that, excepting the martyrs, all canonized Saints, whether belonging to the contemplative, the active or the mixed state, have enjoyed mystic prayer, and normally very exalted forms of it. If, then, it seems almost a prerequisite of heroic virtue, why should we not desire it ? Our Lord has said " Be ye perfect," and He added, what no human person could have dared to add : " as your heavenly Father is perfect." He places before our eyes the perfection of God Himself as our supreme ideal, and, in another saying, He gives us His own meekness and humility as the pattern we are to follow. Perhaps, if these sayings were less familiar, their boldness would take our breath away—and maybe, also, our pusillanimity. We think it presumptuous to aspire to the mystic union—but then what shall we say to Our Lord's demands to be as perfect as the Father and as humble as the Son ? Should we, like the rich youth, turn back in despair at being presented with such unattainable standards ?

God does not demand the impossible. In order to enable us to strive even after Divine perfection He has planted in our hearts a Divine seed—the seed of sanctifying grace, and with it the whole supernatural organism of the virtues and the gifts. It is true, we bear this inestimable treasure in earthen vessels, and, by our own fault, we hardly know that it is there, waiting to unfold itself. We place our light under a bushel, instead of setting it on a candlestick to lighten the household of the faith. " If thou didst know the gift of God . . . thou wouldest have asked of Him, and He would have given thee living water. . . ." The mystics have known both the gift and the boundless munificence of the Giver, who desires to bestow it even now as lovingly as He desired it by the well in Samaria. If we but knew the gift of God, and had the confidence of St. Paul in Him " who is powerful to do superabundantly above all we ask or think, according to the power that operates in us," that is according to the life of grace energising our whole being if we will but let it do so ! If we but knew how to use our supernatural powers, we should also live that mystic union with God, though on a lower plane, that made of a Bernard, a Catherine, a Teresa or a John of the Cross the Saints they were, to the glory of God and of the Mystical Body which is the Church.

CHAPTER I

COUNSELLORS OF POPES AND KINGS

The Power of Sanctity : St. Bernard of Clairvaux

This, to me, is the sublimest philosophy : to know Jesus, and Him crucified.

AT the beginning of the golden age of medieval Christendom stands the towering figure of a monk. Wherever there were difficulties to be settled, controversies to be decided, heretics to be tracked down or injustices to be brought to light, Bernard, Abbot of Clairvaux, was asked for help. He wrote to Popes and Cardinals, kings and princes—letters of appeal, letters of reproach ; there was none so highly placed or so powerful as to be beyond the reach of him who was the living voice of the conscience of Europe. Bernard the arbiter of Church and Empire, Bernard the preacher and miracle worker of the Second Crusade, Bernard the founder of a multitude of monasteries, reformer of old Orders and inspirer of new ones—enough activities, surely, to fill many more than one short life, the life of one, moreover, whose health was all but broken. And yet all this was but the exterior expression of another life, the intense life of Bernard the mystic, who, rapt in contemplation, rode along the Lake of Constance without seeing the water, and who preached those sublime Sermons on the Canticle of Canticles that are one of the greatest glories of Christian mysticism.

One Christmas night, when he was a small boy, he fell asleep while he was waiting for the Night Office to begin. He had a dream vision, in which he saw Mary and the Holy Child, and he understood that it was the very moment of His Birth. As the inaugural visions of the Old Testament prophets sound the theme of their ministry, so the first visions of the Saints often point to what is to be the centre of their inner life. St. Bernard is the mystic of the Sacred Humanity *par excellence*, and whether the "*Jesu dulcis memoria*" and the "*O clemens, o pia, o dulcis Maria*" of the *Salve Regina* are actually by him or not—they express perfectly the spirit, the life-blood of his mysticism, aflame with the love of Jesus and Mary, and their great family, the Church.

Bernard, this son of a noble house of French warriors, was of almost feminine sensibility and strong emotions. Such temperaments are an easy prey to temptation, unless they be prevented by Divine grace and governed by a strong will. St. Bernard had his share of both in a measure far surpassing that of ordinary mortals. When, overcome with grief at the death of his much beloved mother, he attempted to allay his sorrow by worldly distractions, he began for the first time to feel the power of woman. And he realized that for ardent natures like his there are but two ways : the glories and delights of the world, or the utter surrender to God. He knew what to choose : but that his surrender should have brought the very world that he had to give up to his feet so completely as no secular ambition could have dreamt was one of those gifts of the Divine bounty promised by Him who said : Seek ye first the Kingdom of God and its justice, and all these things shall be added unto you.

Bernard never did things by halves. When he had decided to give himself to God he did not choose a monastery like the rich and important Cluny. He deliberately selected the smallest and poorest monastery he could find—Cîteaux, with its handful of half-starved monks who had almost resolved to give up their venture when he presented himself for admission. Nor did he come alone. He, who was to be known in the Church as the "mellifluous doctor," had, by his eloquence and charm, induced thirty of his family and friends to come with him to share the privations of one of the austerest Orders in the Church.

Like all the mystics, he had only one desire : to hide himself, and *Ama nesciri*, love to be unknown, was his watchword—like many of the greatest, he was not permitted to remain hidden. He entered Cîteaux in 1112—in 1115 he was already chosen to be the abbot of a new foundation, by whose name he was to be known all through Christendom. But as yet this born leader of men was lacking in that virtue without which much harm can be done in the spiritual life : the discretion that comes by experience. Like St. Teresa after him he had to learn it through the sufferings of a long illness, which left its traces for the rest of his life. When, in 1119, he returned to the duties of his office, he was weakened in body but matured in mind, ready for the great work that God had chosen him to do.

Soon afterwards he performed his first miracle, and probably about 1121 he wrote his first treatise, *De Gradibus Humilitatis et Superbiae*. It is significant that the first work of the first great mystic of the Middle Ages should have humility for its subject. In the course of these essays we shall have cause to return to it again and again. For humility is the foundation of the mystic life ; and a mysticism that is not firmly built on this foundation is illusion. In the opening chapter of his work Bernard quotes the crucial text, the command given by Our Lord Himself : *Discite a me, quia mitis sum et humilis corde.* For the prayer of the mystics is powerful enough to pierce the clouds precisely because they are humble as Our Lady was humble, and the Lord *respexit humilitatem ancillae suae*. At the threshold of medieval monasticism St. Benedict proposed to his sons his twelve steps of humility, as St. Bernard points out " not in order to enumerate, but to ascend them," for as he says in the Sermons on the Canticle, " unless built on a firm foundation of humility the spiritual edifice can in no wise stand." And what is humility ? " The virtue by which a man despises himself through perfect self-knowledge." In this " cell of self-knowledge," as St. Catherine of Siena will call it over two centuries later, man must dwell if he wants to know God. *Noverim me noverim Te*—there is no other way to the heights of Divine Love but through the valley of self-knowledge, and the more profound the humility of the mystic the more exalted will be his contemplation.

St. Bernard teaches that humility leads to the knowledge of truth, the truth of our own misery, which is the mother of compassion for our neighbour, which in its turn leads the soul thus purified to Divine contemplation. For contemplation is the culmination of the Christian life ; it is to contemplation that he wishes to guide his sons, and to this end he resolved, about fifteen years later, to give his monks those wonderful Sermons on the Canticle of Canticles, which contain the flower of his maturest mystical thought.

It is almost easier to say what these sermons are not than what they are. They are not a theological statement of what contemplation is, as are St. Thomas's articles on the subject in the *Summa*. Nor are they revelations like St. Catherine's *Dialogue ;* nor again an objective account of the ascent of the soul to God in the manner of St. John of the Cross, and even less a description of mystic experiences like the works of St. Teresa. Yet they contain elements of all these. There are passionate outbursts of love, penetrating definitions of mystic states, sublime analyses of the relations between God and the soul—the very richness of the teaching scattered broadcast from the all but inexhaustible treasures of a mind steeped in the teaching of the Bible and the Fathers, and of a soul who has herself attained to the heights of mystic union, almost defies any attempt to give even the most shadowy account of it. For the " mellifluous doctor " was never more filled with sweetness than when he expounded the great love-poem of the Bridegroom and the Bride, Christ and the Church, the Divine Word and the soul.

It is one of the apparent paradoxes of the spiritual life that those who are the humblest of men give most to the innate dignity of the human soul'; whereas the proud and arrogant always evince a profound contempt of their fellows. The solution of this seeming contradiction is their attitude to God. It is the Saint who loves God most and who, knowing by faith that all men are God's children, created and redeemed by Him, loves and venerates them because they are dear to Him whom he loves above all things. The proud man, on the contrary, loves only himself, and therefore uses his fellowmen but as so many instruments for the satisfaction of his own desires. So we see in our time, which began with the proud emancipation of man from the yoke of Him who called Himself " meek and humble of heart," a degradation of man that recalls and perhaps exceeds the worst excesses of pagan slavery. For what is there worthy of respect in the human creature unless it be the Image in which he was made ? There is nothing more staggering, more amazing, more altogether overwhelming than the first mention of man in Scripture : " And God said, let us make man in our image, after our likeness." Because they have been so familiar to us from our childhood we are almost incapable of realizing what these words mean, of seeing that they contain in themselves the solution of the riddle of all the subsequent history of mankind. For the truth which St. Bernard saw so clearly is that man, indeed, is made in the image of God, because he is capable of eternal things, *capax aeternorum*, and that, beyond this, he was also made in the likeness of God, because he was given freedom from sin and freedom from the misery that arises from sin. Because the soul is *ad imaginem Dei* she is *capax Dei*, capable of communing with God. Without the " Image " there would be no common ground, so to speak, on which God and man could meet. The whole edifice of mystic doctrine rests on this foundation. It is true, Christ alone is the Image of Justice, Wisdom and Truth, and " the soul is none of these, because she is not the Image. But she is capable of these and desirous of them, and therefore in the image (*ad imaginem*). An exalted creature, showing forth the sign of majesty in her capacity (of God), and the sign of rectitude in her desire (of God). For it behoves that what is made in an image should correspond with the image, and not bear the name of image in vain." Therefore, man is able to attain union with God, because he is made in His image, and this reflexion of the Divine Word in him can never be destroyed, for it constitutes his very nature.

But whereas the image is inalienable, the " likeness " can be lost, and was actually lost through Adam's disobedience. Yet, by the ineffable mercy of God, it was restored by the Divine act of obedience in the Passion and Death of the Son of God, at the remembrance of which St. Bernard breaks out into transports of love, " Amiable above all things thou hast become unto me, O Good Jesus, through the Chalice which Thou didst drink, the work of our redemption." Through this man, made in the image of God, will also regain the likeness, the *similitudo*, the freedom from sin and its consequences by " putting on Christ," and thus return from the " region of dissimilitude " into his native land of similitude. Therefore, the whole mystic life is nothing but an ever more effective restoration of the lost likeness until man can say with St. Paul, " I live, yet no longer I, but Christ in me."

This work of restoration is the work of love. Several years before he preached the Sermons Bernard had been asked why and in what measure God should be loved ; and in his treatise *De Diligendo Deo* had given the classic answer that " the proper motive for loving God is that He is God, and the measure in which to love Him is to love Him without measure." But how can fallen man attain to these heights ? The restoration of the likeness through love is a slow process of growth, traced by St. Bernard through four stages. Corrupt human nature begins with self-love. But once it has been converted it proceeds to realize its own misery, and in order to escape it the soul turns to God for help. At this stage of the spiritual life man already loves God, but almost entirely for selfish reasons. Yet this love is gradually purified, until God is loved for Himself, though also for the soul's own sake. The element of self-interest is still present and admits of an almost infinite variety of shades—even in the Saints it is never altogether eliminated, though they come already here on earth very near to the fourth stage, which in its purity is reserved for the blessed in heaven, the stage, that is, when man loves even himself only for God's sake. "Happy the man," says St. Bernard, "who has merited to attain to this fourth stage, when he loves not even himself save only for God."

Bernard himself was no doubt nearer to this blessed state than his humility allowed him to admit. He has sung the praises of Divine Love with such burning ardour as only perfect self-surrender can give, and it is hard to doubt that he depicted his own soul when he wrote : "She loves chastely indeed, who only seeks Him whom she loves, and nothing beside Him. In holy manner she loves, not in carnal desire, but in purity of spirit. Ardently also she loves, who is so inebriated with love that she no longer regards the majesty of the Beloved."

Who is this Beloved, whose majesty is forgotten in the burning flames of desire ? It is the Kiss of Divinity and Humanity, which is Christ. "Let him kiss me with the kiss of his mouth " (Cant. 1.1). "For I do not presume," interprets Bernard, the mystic of the Incarnation, "that I should be kissed by His mouth, for this is the unique felicity and the singular prerogative of the assumed Manhood ; but humbly I ask to be kissed with the kiss of His mouth. Mark well, the Word Who assumes humanity is the kissing mouth ; that which is kissed is the flesh which is assumed ; but the Kiss itself is the Person of both the mediator between God and man, the Man Christ Jesus." And he goes on to develop this simile of the Kiss in connection with the threefold way of the inner life ; the kiss of the Feet for the penitent, the kiss of the Hand for those who bring fruit in good works, but the kiss of the Mouth for the perfect, for the contemplatives.

This love of the Incarnate Son which begins with purgation, continues with illumination and is made perfect in union, must be a strong, full, truly human love, an image of the love of Christ. "Learn, Christian," says Bernard, "from Christ how to love Christ. Learn to love sweetly, to love prudently, to love strongly. . . . Let thy soul be inflamed by charity, conformed by knowledge, confirmed by constancy. Let it be fervent, circumspect, and invincible. . . . Let the Lord Jesus be sweet to thy affection, but let Him also be the guiding light to intellect and reason, and let thy love be strong, neither giving way to fears nor succumbing to labours. Let us, therefore, love affectionately, circumspectly, and valiantly." This is another aspect of the threefold way of the spiritual life. The soul of the beginner is attracted by the sweetness of the Lord whom she begins to love with a carnal, emotional love. Such was the love of St. Peter, when he wanted to prevent the Passion. This love must be enlightened so that it will know the things that are profitable—and such was the love of Peter when he offered to follow Our Lord to death, but was yet lacking the strength to carry out what he knew was right. And lastly, love, affectionate and enlightened, must also become valiant, and so was Peter's love when he resisted the Jews, after the Resurrection and the Coming of the Holy Ghost, when he had passed through carnal and rational to spiritual love, *spiritualis amor*.

Now, as the highest stage of the life of prayer, the " kiss of the mouth " which signifies contemplation, corresponds to the highest stage on the way of love—for contemplation is pre-eminently the prayer of love—it follows that in the contemplative love is not only affectionate and illumined, but also made strong by valour. For the contemplative has a special need of valour, since his life is full of vicissitudes and trials. Again and again St. Bernard insists on the transitoriness of contemplation. *Heu! rara hora, et parva mora.* " Alas, rare is the hour, and brief its stay." As long as we are in this life we can only have it partially and for a short time—*ex parte tamen, idque ad tempus, et tempus modicum.* It is true, we cannot attain to it by our own efforts, but we can prepare for it " by vigils, by prayers, by much labour and a shower of tears." Then, when we have so ardently sought Him, He will come—and suddenly, just as we sought to hold Him, He will once more vanish—to come again at the sight of our tears, only to escape, as it were, from our hands, *quasi e manibus evolat.* " Thus, even in this body, the Spouse will often bestow the happiness of His Presence, but not plentifully ; for though His visitation delights, its vicissitudes sadden." These absences, these vicissitudes, are the greatest trials in the life of the mystic, and St. Bernard knows only one remedy : to knock and ask persistently enough to bring back the Beloved, for His absences, he says, are meant to make us seek Him more eagerly.

Yet despite its vicissitudes and trials, the chief characteristic of the contemplative life is a profound peace. St. Bernard has much to say upon this gift, bestowed by Our Lord on His disciples : "Peace I leave unto you, My peace I give unto you." "There is a place," says the Saint, "where God is perceived, truly resting and restful, the place not of the Judge, nor of the Master, but of the Spouse. O place of true quietude, which not without reason, I think, is called the bedchamber. . . . That vision terrifies not, it soothes ; it excites no restless curiosity, but it calms ; nor does it fatigue the senses, but tranquillizes. Here is true rest. The tranquil God tranquillizes all things, and to behold Him is to rest." These are the moments of recompense for past suffering and of strength-gathering for future trials, when God "deigns to appear not as terrible nor as admirable, but as amiable, serene and benign, sweet and meek." And what should the soul do when the Spouse thus visits her ? St. Bernard gives the same answer as, some 400 years later, St. John of the Cross : "If it should so happen that one of you be some time ravished and concealed in this hidden sanctuary of God, let him in no wise be called away nor be disturbed, whether by the needs of the senses or by consuming cares, nor by gnawing guilt—nor indeed by this unrest, so difficult to keep out, of the corporal pictures of the imagination."

For contemplation is a form of sleep—an expression frequently used by St. Bernard, but which must be rightly understood. "How great and stupendous an honour," he says, "that He should make the contemplating soul rest in His bosom, and that, moreover, he should guard her from irritating cares, protect her from disquieting activity and worrying business, nor suffer her to be awakened save by her own will." The "sleep," then, is only a rest from the haunting preoccupations of daily life and their reflexions in the unceasing play of the imagination—but, looked at from another point of view, it is intensest action, action than which nothing could be more fruitful, nothing more satisfying, because it is the action of God on the soul, stimulating and fertilizing all her powers, and the mere remembrance of it makes Bernard overflow with happiness and gratitude : "I am beside myself with joy that to incline to so familiar and sweet intercourse with our infirmity such Majesty should not disdain . . . what, thinkest thou, shall she receive in heaven, who here on earth is granted such familiarity that by God's arms she feels herself embraced, in God's bosom

B

cherished, by God's care and zeal guarded lest she, asleep, should
be, unwilling, roused, before she waketh by herself. . . . For truly
this is slumber, which, however, not numbs sense, but withdraws
it. . . . And, therefore, not absurdly would I call death the
spouse's ecstasy, though it does not ravish life, but the snares of
life," which, however, need not be feared "as often as by a holy
and vehement thought the soul is drawn out of herself, in mind
she secedes and escapes so far that she transcends the use and habit
of thought. . . ." And in this upper region, above the ordinary
functions of discursive human reason, she is freed, not, indeed,
from life, but from the sensation of life and from its temptations.
For in the flight of ecstasy she has transcended the limitations of
the body, the region of dissimilitude, and therefore is at rest ;
Quis dabit mihi pennas sicut columbae, et volabo et requiescam ?

Yet, this ecstasy of peace which lifts the mystic above the turmoil
of human thought and which is the mark of all genuine contemplation, is always marvellously adapted to our individual requirements which are different for every soul : " For the various needs
of the soul," he writes, " the taste of the Divine Presence must
necessarily vary, and the infused taste of supernal sweetness will
delight the spiritual palate in diverse manners according to the
various desires of each." This is the reason of the rich variety of
the life of grace, as varied as, or even more so than, the life of
nature. Both, grace and nature, have their great laws of development which are but rarely set aside. Yet, within this framework
of law and order there is infinite variety, telling of the infinite
riches of the Creator of both. And this Creator, who knows the
needs of all His creatures, lavishes on His contemplatives all those
helps required by their frail human nature, which cannot bear the
full light of the Godhead while they are in this body. Therefore,
" at once—I know not whence—there are present certain imaginary
similitudes of inferior things, conveniently adapted to the divinely
infused thoughts by which that most pure and luminous ray of
truth is in some measure overshadowed, so that it becomes more
tolerable to the soul herself and more intelligible to those to whom
she wants to communicate it." For contemplation is not only an
excessus of love, it is also an illumination of the intellect.

It is one of the surest signs of genuine ecstasy that, though its
outward manifestations may often resemble a swoon, the soul
is inundated with supernatural light, and under the influence

of the Gifts of the Holy Ghost is filled with wisdom and understanding ; for "when the Spirit speaks, falsehood and doubt pass
away, and there is not only Truth, but the certainty of Truth."
When the fire of love has consumed the stains of sin, and when
the conscience is purified and at peace, there follows "a certain
sudden and unwonted enlarging of the mind, an infusion of light
enlightening the intellect unto the knowledge of the Scriptures
or the understanding of mysteries—the one, so it seems to me,
given for our own delectation, the other for the edification of
our neighbour." For it is but fitting that the soul who is the spouse
of the Divine Word should participate, however imperfectly,
"not through open gates, but through narrow ravines"—in
the uncreated wisdom to whom she is espoused, for "God is
wisdom, and He desires to be loved not only sweetly, but wisely,'
therefore, "it is not right that the spouse of the Word should be
stupid."

Thus in the mystic charity and wisdom interact ; love is
inflamed by understanding, understanding is illumined by love,
and under the powerful influence of both the contemplative
attains at last to the fulness of his vocation : he becomes a bowl
overflowing with Divine plenitude, which from its fulness can
give to others without diminishing its own contents. St. Bernard
has but scorn and reproof for "pipes"—canales—as he calls those
teachers who, as soon as they have received a tiny bit for themselves
are eager, like pipes, to give out as quickly as they can the little
that was meant for their own profit—being left empty themselves
and useless to others. "If you are wise, he says, you will show
yourself a bowl, not a pipe. For a pipe gives out almost as quickly
as it has received, but the bowl waits until it is filled, and then
if there be a surplus, it communicates without loss." In this the
contemplative must imitate none other than God Himself, Who
lives in the fulness of His own Divine Life, and "thus overflowing
with many mercies visits the earth."

St. Bernard in no way belittles the life of action—like St.
Thomas after him, he regards the "mixed life," the contemplata
aliis tradere, as the highest vocation. But action must be an overflow of contemplation, rooted in charity, not an aimless activism
springing from ambition. meddlesomeness and such like motives.
"For true and chaste contemplation, he says, sometimes so fills
the mind, vehemently inflamed by Divine zeal, with eagerness

and longing to give souls to God who love Him in like manner, that it will gladly interrupt the rest of contemplation for preaching." Neither will harm the other ; for contemplation will give depth to preaching, and preaching in its turn will enrich contemplation. The great difficulty is to keep the right balance between the two. How can poor fallible man achieve the ideal of neither sacrificing works of charity to the delights of contemplation nor neglecting contemplation out of zeal for his neighbour ? " The only remedy, replies St. Bernard, is to pray that He may deign always to show us what, when and in what wise He wishes us to act." *Praedicatio, oratio, contemplatio*—these three constitute the spiritual life in its perfection, typefied by Martha who ministered, Lazarus " as it were sighing under the stone and imploring the grace of resurrection," and Mary sitting at the feet of Jesus. No one human life will be rich enough to have all three in perfection, but they must all be present at least in intention. Action, prayer, contemplation, typefied by the family whom Jesus loved—such is the ideal that Bernard sets before his monks. Such, too, is the ideal that he realised in his own life in a fulness granted only to the very greatest in the Kingdom of Heaven, to a St. Dominic and a St. Francis, to a St. Catherine of Siena and a St. Teresa. Contemplation, prayer and action—in this great triad lies the secret of the vitality of the Saints and of the ever-fresh vigour of the Church. One without the other two is barren, but the three together are infinitely fruitful. Therefore, " every man is deemed perfect in whose soul these three harmoniously meet : he who knows how to sigh for himself, to exult in God, and to assist his neighbour in his needs."

St. Hildegard

SHORTLY after 1141 St. Bernard received a letter from a Bene- dictine nun at Bingen consulting him on the subject of visions and revelations which she had received. His reply was very cautious—saying little on what she wanted to hear, but inculcating the practice of the Christian virtues, the solid foundations of the spiritual life for every one, whether favoured with visions and other extraordinary phenomena or not. In all probability the nun received the snub with humility, for she was not only one of the most remarkable women of the Middle Ages, but also a great Saint.

It is often believed, even by Catholics, that in the " Dark " Ages of Faith women were kept under lock and key, in abysmal ignorance of anything but cooking and childbearing, and that only the " emancipation " of the nineteenth century put an end to their slavery. History, however, tells us exactly the opposite. When Europe was still united in one Faith, the Church allowed no man to forget that God was born of a woman ; and after Our Lady she honoured holy virgins and widows, martyrs and penitents. Was she likely to despise the living, who were so many potential saints ? It is true, she kept St. Paul's injunction : *Mulier taceat in Ecclesia*—but this silence was strictly confined to the Church as the place of the Divine Sacrifice—everywhere else she was allowed to raise her voice, even to reproach priests, bishops, and the Pope himself.

St. Hildegard of Bingen belongs to that spiritual family of valiant women from which came St. Catherine of Siena and St. Joan of Arc, the holy German Empress Adelheid and the first Christian dramatist of Europe, Hrotsvith of Gandersheim. She was born at Spanheim, in the Palatinate, towards the close of the eleventh century. She had her first vision at the tender age of three, and entered the religious life at the Benedictine convent of Mount Disibode when she was eight. Her visions and revelations continued throughout her life, and her advice was eagerly sought by persons from all ranks of society. Perhaps her most remarkable correspondent was the German Emperor Frederick Barbarossa whom, as most of her other clients, including the higher clergy and the Pope, she vigorously exhorted to mend his life and do penance. The proud Emperor, autocratic and self-willed though he was, bowed before the spiritual authority of the humble nun whose exhortations were accompanied by predictions that came true.

St. Hildegard evidently had the gift of prophecy in a remarkable degree. The punishments she foretold for the negligence of the clergy have often been thought to refer to the Reformation. Speaking in the person of the Church, the Saint thus warns the priests : " The princes and peoples will fall upon you, priests, who have neglected me for so long ; they will cast you off and put you to flight, and take away your riches because you have not fulfilled the duties of your priestly office." This concise description certainly fits the events of the Reformation exactly. To quote the Bollandist editor of her works : "If there is any person in the Middle Ages who, according to the judgment of many authorities, is certain to have enjoyed divine revelations, it is St. Hildegard." For three Popes, Eugenius III, Anastasius IV and Hadrian IV, as well as the Council of Trèves were agreed that her revelations were true and that her doctrine came from God.

St. Hildegard herself claimed that all her knowledge was infused and came to her in visions. As a matter of fact the visionary state was, as it were, normal to her, beginning at the age of three and remaining with her throughout her life. This is how she describes it : "I see my visions not in dreams, or sleeping, or in my brain (*in phrenesi*), nor with my bodily eyes or the ears of the outer man, nor in hidden places ; but I have received them ʼʰⁱⁿg, looking round—according to the will of God—in a pure mind with the eyes and ears of the inner man, openly." Her visions, then, differ in many respects from those of other mystics — anyway this kind of visions, for there was another which will be discussed later. They were not, as in the case of St. Teresa, for example, transitory, but an uninterrupted state. They were not accompanied by abnormal physical phenomena such as trance or levitation. They were, on the contrary, as ordinary as things seen by her bodily eyes and did not hinder her usual occupations—there seems to have been no trace of "ligature." When, as a child, she first discovered that other people did not see the things she saw she was deeply distressed, and from that time hid them carefully from all except her spiritual advisers and confidants.

She describes this visionary state as a light which she always sees in her soul, a light that is not in a place, and is far brighter than a cloud through which the sun shines, and which has "neither height nor length nor breadth. And this is called the shadow of the living light (*umbra viventis luminis*). And just as sun, moon and stars appear in the water, so scriptures and sermons, virtues, and certain deeds of men I see reflected in it. And whatever I see or learn in that vision I remember for a long time . . . but what I do not see thus, that I know not, for I am, as it were, illiterate." This "light" in which she saw things appears to have been a phenomenon similar to that of the "mystic sun" of Bl. Anna Maria Taigi, who also saw the future or things that were happening at a distance in a supernatural light without ecstasy or trance. It seems as if these extraordinary gifts which enable their recipients to advise others in the most difficult situations are granted especially to those called to a particular work in the Church, for which they are not fitted by their natural gifts and position. A nun of a small Benedictine monastery—or a poor Italian housewife—these are not the persons whom we should expect to be counsellors of Popes and kings. But God has His own methods to bring home to the world that Divine Wisdom depends not on human learning, and that He can make known mysteries to the humble that are inaccessible to scholars. From St. Hildegard's descriptions it would almost seem as if all her knowledge came to her in the same way as it comes to the blessed in Heaven who see all things in God, excepting, of course, the Beatific Vision itself. Yet, as Père Poulain remarks : " It is impossible to admit that all that this Saint wrote came from God. For her works are full of scientific errors, and exactly those errors that were prevalent in the twelfth century " (*The Graces of Interior Prayer*, ch. xxi). On the other hand, it is a fact that she had never learnt Latin and yet knew the sense of passages from the Bible and the Fathers which she was reading, and even dictated in that language with the help of a secretary who corrected the grammar. Though we may admit that she probably " picked up " more than she herself realised from books and conversations, the supernatural origin of her knowledge can hardly be denied —not only because there is no reason to doubt her own testimony but also because, as we shall see, her mystic doctrine is always in strict accordance with the greatest doctors that came after her, especially St. Thomas and St. John of the Cross.

But if most of her knowledge was, indeed, infused, why was she allowed to deceive herself and to regard as Divine Truth what was but the erroneous hypothesis of her day ? Père Poulain offers a solution of this difficult problem : " In order to explain in a favourable light St. Hildegard's illusions on scientific subjects, we may admit the following hypothesis : God, it seems, may supernaturally convey into a person's mind a portion of the knowledge of the day . . . whilst giving in some way a general warning that He does not guarantee the contents of the whole and that it is, therefore, to be accepted only at the receiver's risk." Ingenious though this hypothesis may be, it seems to us that it places a certain lack of veracity in God in order to exonerate the Saint. To us it would appear simpler to admit that Hildegard though supernaturally enlightened on all matters pertaining to her own spiritual life and the salvation of her neighbour, was permitted to deceive herself on subjects not connected with either, so that in all good faith she attributed to Divine illumination what came to her through human channels. Such an admixture of error is not infrequent in the lives of the mystics and detracts in no way from the value of their spiritual doctrine ; whereas a supernatural infusion of faulty natural knowledge would seem to us to raise quite unnecessarily grave theological problems.

Apart from her, as it were "normal", visionary state just described, St. Hildegard enjoyed another kind of vision which, however, was rare. "Sometimes," she tells us, "I see in this (the ' ordinary ') light another light, which is called the living light. Whilst I behold this light all sadness and sorrow leave my memory, so that I feel like a young girl, and not like an elderly woman." It is always misleading to apply a hard and fast terminology to the different mystic states of different souls. It is, however, obvious that the Saint here gives a description of infused contemplation properly so called, in which the impression of light is frequently present to the imagination, and which is—except in the case of "arid" contemplation—always accompanied by great peace and a sense of well-being and contentment. She describes one of these states, which were quite different from her ' ordinary ' visions, in much the same manner as St. Teresa does her ecstasies : "I saw a mystic and wondrous vision," she says, "so that all my inner parts were shaken, and the sensibility of my body was extinguished ; my consciousness was turned into another mode as if I knew not myself." This is something essentially different from that other state in which she normally received her revelations. Here we have a clear description of ecstasy with its physical accompaniment of loss of sensibility and a change of the ordinary mode of perception by reasoning into supernatural illumination, whereas in the other state the Saint saw but "the shadow of the living light" and acquired knowledge by supernatural means, without any signs of being in a state of mystic prayer. It is one more proof of the divine origin of most of her visions that she herself knew the apparently so much more " supernatural " gift of prophecy to be of an inferior order—in full accord with the Thomist doctrine of the superiority of sanctifying grace to the *gratiae gratis datae* of prophecy and other extraordinary gifts.

This differentiation between prophetic visions and mystic contemplation is reflected in St. Hildegard's written work, especially in the *Scivias*.

The bulk of the *Scivias*, which, we are told, were written at the express command of God, contains very elaborate descriptions of visions comparable in form to those of the prophet Ezechiel and of St. John. They are always followed by minute allegorical interpretations which are often combined with moral exhortations. Thus, in the First Vision of the *Scivias*, the Saint sees One sitting on a mountain—which denotes the stability of the Kingdom of God—denouncing the tepidity of men. She sees in these visions angels and animals, stars and rivers, Anti-Christ and the Woman— but these are externals. In the often fantastic descriptions there is enshrined pure Christian doctrine on an amazing variety of subjects, showing a theological insight that, in an unlettered woman, can only have been due to special revelation.

Perhaps the most astonishing fact is the absence of all emotion in these visions. They are permeated with a deep love of God and zeal for souls, but a love that has its seat entirely in the will, not in the feelings. In vain do we look for descriptions of loving intercourse between Christ and the soul such as abound in the lives of St. Gertrude or St. Margaret Mary. With the great medieval Benedictine all is restraint and austerity. Her life is dominated by the knowledge that man is an *animal rationale*, and that the intellect is God's loftiest gift to him. In the midst of her visionary world of allegorical beings she rings the changes on this great theme as if she were a disciple of the Angelic Doctor. " But thou, O man, sayest, I cannot do good. But I say, thou canst. Thou askest : how ? I answer : By intellect and reason." The Saint does not, of course, teach that man can do good on his own account. It is God who works in him. But in truly Thomist manner she explains that God has constituted man in such a way that He works through the human reason which He has given man for the express purpose of showing him " what is good and what evil."

She insists on the freedom of the will as if she were answering an imaginary Luther or Karl Barth, or those modern psychologists who would persuade us that we must follow our inclinations wherever they may lead us. " But if you say you cannot do good works, that you say in your iniquity. For you have eyes to see, ears to hear, a heart to think, hands to work and feet to walk . . . thus has God created you. Wherefore also resist the desires of your flesh and God will help you."

" Resist the desires of your flesh. . . ." St. Hildegard, like all true mystics, knew how indispensable is asceticism to the Christian life. She calls it the " Mother of virtue," and places it at the beginning of the *Via Mystica*. Her mysticism, like her doctrinal teaching, is austere, and much of it reads like an anticipation of St. John of the Cross. In the fourth vision of the *Scivias* she gives a wonderful description of the Mystic Way. The soul, seeking her lost home, asks the eternal question of man : " Where am I wanderer ? " And she is answered : " In the shadow of death." Again : " In what way do I walk ? In the way of error. Which consolation have I ? The comfort of a wanderer." Then, far away, she hears the call of Sion, her Mother, the call to the life of prayer. She follows the voice, but the way is hard, and she nearly gives up the venture, when her Mother tells her that God has given her wings to fly. So now she need no longer walk in the arduous way of meditation, she realizes that she will be borne on the wings of contemplation, a metaphor loved by the mystics ; later, St. Teresa will develop it in her simile of the caterpillar which is transformed into a butterfly. Then the soul takes courage and, strengthened by contemplative prayer, she comes to a " taber-nacle," where she is protected from the arrows of her enemies. This " tabernacle " probably means something like Master Eckhart's *Castellum* and St. Teresa's inner mansions of her *Interior Castle*, namely, the inner sanctuary of the soul where God Himself dwells. Outward temptations cannot follow her there, but the devil now uses subtler weapons, firing her thirst for knowledge and her ambition. This attack, too, is overcome, and the soul begins at last to walk in the way of godliness. And now she enters on a yet higher way, to which she is introduced by purgations which clearly correspond to the " Night of the Spirit " of St. John of the Cross. " I wish," she writes, " to ascend beyond my intellect and to begin what I cannot accomplish. But when I attempt this a great sorrow comes over me, so that I perform no work in high sanctity nor in the fulness of good will, but feel nothing within myself but the unrest of doubt and despair. Wherefore also this iniquity attacks me that all happiness, all good both in man and God becomes wearisome and distasteful to me."

The ascent above the intellect into the realm of the Divine which cannot be apprehended by human reason is necessarily accompanied by suffering, and this suffering has extraordinary purifying powers, for it makes man see his own iniquity in a way in which he could never have realized it without these passive purgations. The Divine light shows up the darkness of human sin with a startling clarity in which, what has before seemed trifling, now assumes terrifying proportions. " I appear to myself," Hildegard writes, " in the inner part of my soul as ashes of ashes, and as dust in my instability, therefore I sit trembling like a feather. But do not cut me off from the land of the living, because in the vileness of my stupidity I think myself in the lowest and vilest place so that I am not worthy to be called human."

Most mystics use similar language when they speak of their own shortcomings, which, to us, seems exaggerated. Yet it is not their, but our point of view that is distorted. We are so blinded by sin that we fail to perceive the hideousness of even the smallest fault in the eyes of the Divine holiness, which will become manifest to us only on the day of which the Church sings : *Quid sum miser tunc dicturus . . . cum vix justus sit securus.* Only in the flames of Purgatory will most of us learn the true meaning of sin— but the mystics have known it already on earth, therefore, they cannot find words strong enough to express their horror at their own failings that seem so insignificant to us. *Quid sum miser tunc dicturus . . .* if the Saints speak thus of themselves. There is, however, one consolation. The purifications are the more intense, the higher the degree of sanctity to which a soul is predestined. There are many mansions in heaven, and from those who have received less, God will demand less—though it is dangerous to be satisfied with little when eternal salvation is at stake. The mystics are not so easily satisfied, they ask for much—but like the man who desired the pearl of great price they are ready to give all they have to obtain it.

St. Hildegard knows that intense purification is necessary for

her perfection. For God has revealed to her that He casts men
into desolation "thus taking away from them their elation, nor
permitting them to know what hidden good is in them, because
I want to produce much fruit in them." Without this pruning
there can be no true mysticism, for man tainted by sin cannot
reach the heights of union with God without profound suffering
in the depths of his nature which has to be cleansed from the last
vestiges of pride and self-will. In the darkness of this "night"
the soul learns true humility, and humility, says St. Hildegard,
is to charity what the body is to the soul, they can never be separated
in this life. For God is apprehended in faith by a contrite heart,
there is no other mode of knowing Him while we live in this body,
whatever heights our spiritual life may have reached. St. Hildegard
is very clear on this ; she knew she received extraordinary graces
to be accepted with humility, but she also knew the difference
between the order of grace and the order of glory, for, like all
the mystics, she had received the gift of wisdom in an eminent
degree, which enabled her to see her own mystic experiences in
the light of theological truth.

It is probably because the pearls of her wisdom are scattered
here and there among her fantastic descriptions of the things she
saw that St. Hildegard is so little known as a mystic. Yet the
holy Benedictine was a worthy precursor of the great German
mystics of the fourteenth century, St. Mechtild and the three
Dominicans Eckhart, Tauler and Suso, and deserves to be honoured
in their company. Her extraordinary gifts, like those of St.
Catherine of Siena and Blessed Anna Maria Taigi, were used only
for the good of her neighbour and of the Church, and from the
silence of her convent she exercised an influence which, if not
as widespread as that of St. Bernard, was deep and beneficial,
making for the *Pax Benedictina* for which her Order worked so
devotedly among the warring tribes of her people.

St. Catherine of Siena—A Mystic in the World

The soul cannot live without love, but always wants to love something, because she is made for love, and by love I created her.
                                                ST. CATHERINE, *Dialogue.*

IT is one of the most consoling facts that mystics seem to flourish
especially in turbulent times. The graces of contemplative prayer

need but a pure heart in which to take root, however much the world may be torn by wars and unrest. There is no more striking example of the mystic life lived in the turmoil of the world than that of St. Catherine of Siena. Few women have had a more amazing career than this young dyer's daughter, who made her way from the plain little room in her parents' house to the palace of the Popes of Avignon, who braved revolutionary crowds and wrote letters to cardinals and kings, and all through her life preserved her uninterrupted union with God in times perhaps as unsettled as our own. What was it that made such a life possible, what were the doctrines on which it was built ? She herself has given us the answer in her *Dialogue* and *Letters*, which contain a wealth of mystical thought. For it is her mystic life that gives us the explanation of her extraordinary power over men and women, by which she converted criminals on their way to the scaffold and faced the intrigues of the French Cardinals who tried to prevent the Pope's return to Rome.

At the root of her spiritual life, the source of her power, is her doctrine of the " inner cell." This cell, which she herself never left, consists, as it were, of two compartments. They are knowledge of God and knowledge of self, summed up in the great twofold truth by which she was guided : " I am He Who is, and thou art she who is not." This fertile principle of the knowledge of God and of self nourishes man's spiritual life from the first stirrings of Divine Grace to the sublimest heights of the mystic union. At the beginning it is the root of virtue, for through the knowledge of the Divine Omnipotence and the nothingness of the creature the soul is brought to the fear of God, the beginning of wisdom, by which she turns away from those things that displease Him and does those He commands. Then, in gratitude for the benefits received, she begins to increase in the knowledge of God and of herself, and through this knowledge servile fear is gradually transformed into love. For, as God teaches St. Catherine, " the soul should season the knowledge of herself with the knowledge of my goodness," else she might fall into despair.

Yet at this stage her knowledge is far from perfect ; it needs to be purified in temptation. " For one does not arrive at virtue except through knowledge of self, and knowledge of me, which knowledge is more perfectly acquired in the time of temptation, because then man knows himself to be nothing." St. Catherine, though she received the call to perfection in her first vision at the age of six, and made a vow of virginity at seven, knew the power of temptation as only the Saints know it. When she was twelve years old her family decided to marry her, and her elder sister persuaded her to show off her beautiful hair. For a time nature had her way and Catherine made herself look pretty. But grace was not to be conquered by vanity. The future saint learned the transitoriness of all earthly beauty through the sudden death of the same sister who had taught her the female arts of pleasing. Under the impression of that death the vow of the child was renewed by the woman, and the early love of God, tested in temptation, became the full-grown love that is stronger than death. This first temptation was followed by other trials, which taught Catherine that the nothingness of the creature is most deeply experienced when the soul is visited by aridity and desolation. They are the most powerful means by which Divine Providence leads her to perfection, for, said the Lord to her, "This I do so that, coming to perfect self-knowledge, men may know that of themselves they are nothing and have no grace, and accordingly in time of battle fly to me."

Knowledge, then, is the mother of true humility, for it is inconceivable to the saint that a man should truly know himself to be a creature and not be humble. And this knowledge of self brings forth another virtue, patience, which Catherine calls the Queen of virtues and the marrow of charity, for it is " conceived in self-knowledge and in knowledge of my goodness to the souls, and brought forth by means of holy hatred and anointed with true humility." Thus the supernatural life gradually unfolds through knowledge, for it is " in the house of self-knowledge, with holy prayer, where imperfections are lost."

This truly Thomist emphasis on knowledge, which the Tertiary of Siena must have imbibed from her Dominican directors, is complemented by one of her most characteristic doctrines, her teaching on faith as " the pupil of the eye of the intellect," considered by Garrigou-Lagrange the leading idea of her whole life. At a comparatively early stage of her mystic development she asked God for the perfection in faith, and it was granted her in a vision known as her " Espousals." In a mystic festival, in the presence of St. John the Evangelist, St. Paul, St. Dominic and David who played the harp, Our Lady asked her Divine Son to espouse Catherine to Himself in faith ; and in token of the Betrothal she received an invisible ring. With the extraordinary intellectual vigour so characteristic of her spirituality the mystic experience bore fruit in her teaching. However highly she esteems the human intellect capable of showing man his duties, it needs faith as the eye needs the pupil " in order to discern, to know and to follow the way and the doctrine of my truth—the Word incarnate ; and without this pupil of faith the soul would not see." Reason and faith are made for each other and are as inseparable as the pupil is from the eye. When the pupil is destroyed the eye cannot see ; when faith is lost reason falls into error. Thus, when the soul covers the pupil of faith " with the cloth of infidelity, drawn over it by self-love," she no longer sees. Faith has become ineffective and has ceased its mission of illuminating the soul.

It is remarkable that St. Catherine attributes this failure neither to intellectual difficulties nor to bad influences and evil habits, but to the deepest root of all spiritual failure, to love of self—that is, to sin against the First Commandment. Though she was still living in what is commonly called the " ages of Faith," the time of the Avignon Popes and the Great Western Schism was characterized precisely by this loss of the living faith through the inordinate self-love of so many of the Church's members, especially among the higher clergy, which St. Catherine spent her whole life to remedy. For faith, in her language, does not just mean an intellectual assent to the truths of Revelation. Faith for her is a dynamic force that controls the whole Christian life. If to her the weak and vacillating Gregory XI is yet " the Christ on earth," if the lukewarm or even vicious priests are yet the " Ministers of Blood " though they should commit sacrilege at every Mass they offer, it is by the " pupil of the most holy faith " that she discerns behind these miserable human instruments the tremendous spiritual realities they represent. In her letters we read again and again the command : " Open the eye of your intellect " ; for it is to the great truths of the faith that she wants to guide her " spiritual family," as she calls the group of men and women of all ages and stations in life who had gathered round her powerful personality. These truths must be discerned first by the intellect and appropriated by faith in order to be loved by the will and practised in daily life.

Among these truths there is one especially dear to her, to which she recurs again and again, the great saving truth of Redemption in the Precious Blood. Her letters begin almost invariably : " I, Catherine, servant and slave of the servants of Jesus Christ, write to you in His Precious Blood." This mystery of the Redemption she develops in the beautiful simile of the Bridge, revealed to her by God the Father. He teaches her that He has given man the Bridge of His Son " in order that, passing across the flood, you may not be drowned, which flood is the stormy sea of this dark life." On the day of the Ascension this bridge rose from earth to heaven, yet without leaving the earth, for it is made of " the height of the divinity, joined with your humanity." Through the union of both in Christ man can now safely cross the river of life, for the bridge is made of stones which signify the virtues. They were built into the bridge only after the Passion of Our Lord, which released the streams of grace, for heaven was opened " with the key of His Blood." But the Eternal Truth adds a warning, lest man should trust presumptuously in the efficacy of this Blood : " And observe that it is not enough, in order that you should have life, that my Son should have made you this Bridge, unless you also walk on it." And God showed her that " though He created us without ourselves, He would not save us without ourselves."

Yet He knows human weakness, and in His mercy, lest we should faint on the way, He has provided places of refreshment on this Bridge, which are the Sacraments. They were given us to renew our strength and to fit us for the spiritual ascent to which Christ, the Bridge, invites us. For in His crucified Body St. Catherine discerns the three stages of the spiritual life. His pierced Feet symbolize the affections, which must be detached from earthly pleasures in order to become " steps by which thou canst arrive at His Side which manifests to thee the secret of His Heart, because the soul, rising on the steps of her affection, begins to taste the love of His Heart, gazing into that open Heart of my Son." St. Catherine was one of the first mystics to whom, as to St. Gertrude, God revealed the Sacred Heart. It plays, however, a smaller part in her life than in that of the Benedictine Saint. In this passage from the *Dialogue* access to the Sacred Heart symbolizes the second stage of the spiritual life, the illuminative way, in which the soul acquires the virtues. Only when she has passed this second step " the soul reaches out to the third, that is to the mouth where she finds peace from the terrible war she has been waging against her sin."

" Let him kiss me with the kiss of his mouth "—these words have signified to St. Bernard, and, indeed, to generations of Christian mystics, the heights of the spiritual life, the Divine union tasted by the soul who has reached the summits. Though she may still suffer intensely in her lower part, she is established in the peace that surpasses all understanding, in the " ground," the *scintilla animae*, where she receives a foretaste even in this life of the beatitude of the saints in heaven. Thus the " Bridge " of the Incarnate Son is both a safe way to salvation for the multitude of the faithful, and an ascent to the heights of contemplation for those called, like St. Catherine herself, to the summits of the mystic life.

These few characteristic doctrines of the Saint have been pointed out because her life is penetrated probably to a higher degree than that of any other woman mystic by theology. Maxime Gorce calls her " une très grande théologienne " ; but her theology was learned not in the lecture room but in the school of contemplation ; it was, according to the verdict of the Church in the process of her canonization, infused. The infused knowledge of the Saints is a complex thing, as we have already seen in the case of St. Hildegard. It abstracts neither altogether from the natural gifts and inclinations of the subject, nor can it be accounted for by human agencies alone. As regards the first point, St. Catherine was certainly influenced by her Dominican entourage ; her stress on truth and on the importance of the intellect are thoroughly Dominican. On the other hand, her doctrine is of a surety of touch, a theological accuracy and a mystic elevation which would be admirable in a trained theologian but which are altogether marvellous in a young woman of very little education. It cannot be explained except by supernatural illumination, working on the natural data of an unusual intelligence helped by constant intercourse with theologians. For infused knowledge has a certain likeness to artistic inspiration. This, too, presupposes the ordinary groundwork, the technique that can, and indeed must be learned. But in order to produce a real work of art the artist needs " inspiration," a mysterious force that cannot be acquired but is a " gift." Thus also grace, on the natural foundations of human influences and personal leanings, builds up its edifice of infused knowledge

C

by which the contemplative penetrates the mysteries of faith in a manner far more profound and vitalizing than the theologian whose learning is not enlivened by the mystic current.

It has seemed necessary to insist on the intellectual side of St. Catherine's mysticism in order not to be taken aback by the extraordinary states in which her life abounds. For even an expert in spirituality of the rank of a Henri Bremond could prefer the Ursuline Beata Marie de l'Incarnation to the Saint of Siena because, he writes, " Catherine de Sienne pâmée entre les bras de ses compagnes, ne nous scandalise point, mais nous l'aimerions mieux debout." This is a serious misunderstanding which, moreover, applies not only to St. Catherine, but to all mystics whose interior life expresses itself in strange physical phenomena.

The idea of St. Catherine " in a swoon in the arms of her companions " was probably suggested by the well-known picture of Sodoma representing the imprint of the Stigmata. There is, as the remarks of Bremond show, a school of thought that tends to minimize these " extraordinary " graces and to be apologetic about them, as if they were almost disreputable incidents in the lives of the Saints of which the less said the better. This may be a salutary reaction against an unhealthy avidity for these things ; but for all our insistence that the essence of mysticism does not consist in them, we have to remember that the Church, by sanctioning special feasts, e.g., of the Stigmata of St. Francis and of those of St. Catherine, has herself set the seal of approval to the supernatural origin and the high spiritual significance of these states. There is nothing unhealthy or hysterical about the physical conforming of the body to the Body of the crucified Spouse of the soul. It is a well-known phenomenon even in the natural sphere that a long marriage tends to produce a surprising likeness in the features of husband and wife. Thus in the realm of the supernatural God chooses some men and women especially dear to Him and produces in them certain physical likenesses to His Incarnate Life. In St. Catherine's case this physical assimilation even went so far that on one occasion, when her director, Bl. Raymund of Capua, could not believe in the greatness of the revelations granted to her, he suddenly saw her face changed into that of Our Lord, and when, overawed, he asked her who she was, she answered : " I am He Who Is."

It is, indeed, the greatness of the revelations that causes these

phenomena, and St. Catherine's life was particularly rich in them.
One of the most extraordinary among them is that known as her
" mystic death," which was produced by the sudden overpowering
realization of Our Lord's love for souls. At the thought of it her
heart seemed to break, she entered into an agony, and, to all
appearances, lay dead for four hours. According to her own
testimony she enjoyed during these hours something akin to the
Beatific Vision, and at the same time she was shown the pains of
purgatory and hell. When she returned to life she wept three
days with grief at being once more separated from the full union
with her Lord, just as St. Teresa, coming out of her famous " ecstasy
of Salamanca," exclaimed "I die because I cannot die." St.
Catherine's mystic death, which seems in a way to have resembled
St. Paul's great rapture during which he knew not whether he
was " in the body or out of the body," prepared her for a more
intense apostolic life, which had until then be confined mainly
to the nursing of the sick and the visiting of the poor, and inflamed
her with that burning love of souls that was to overcome all
obstacles to her mission and convert the most hardened sinners.
For such extraordinary graces are almost always given for others,
and they have to be bought invariably by suffering.

The sufferings of the Saints are of those mysterious realities
that can be understood only in the light of the Passion of Christ.
The mystics' thirst for suffering, so conspicuous in their lives,
yet so unintelligible to human nature, is a sign of their intimate
union with the Lord who said to His disciples : " If any man will
come after me let him deny himself and take up his cross and follow
me." St. Catherine had her full share in this Cross, in illness and
slander, in opposition and misunderstandings. But what weighed
most heavily on her and what was most intimately connected with
her mystic life was the state of the Church, " the Spouse of Christ "
as she loves to call her, corrupted by the vices of the clergy and soon
to be torn by schism. When this Great Western Schism, which
she had long foreseen, became a reality, her ardent love impelled
her to make the supreme sacrifice and to offer her life for the
Church. " Then the devils called out havoc upon me, seeking
to hinder and slacken with their terrors my free and burning desire.
So they beat upon the shell of the body ; but desire became the
more kindled, crying : O Eternal God, receive the sacrifice of my
life in this mystical body of Holy Church ! I have nothing to

give Thee save what Thou hast given to me. Take then my heart and press it out over the face of Thy Spouse." Her desire was fulfilled to the letter. From that time until her death the remaining months of her life were one long agony of physical and spiritual torments. " This body of mine remains without any food, without even a drop of water ; in such tortures as I never at any time endured. . . . In this way, and many others which I cannot tell, my life is consumed and shed for this sweet Bride. I by this road, and the glorious martyrs by blood."

Thus, at the end of her life, St. Catherine was perfectly conformed to her Lord by the mystery of vicarious suffering. She had throughout the period of her apostolic activities performed terrifying penances and endured intense sufferings on behalf of sinners. But now she did it all for the Church as a whole and in obedience to a formal command from God, who, in answer to her anxious question : " What can I do, O unsearchable fire ?", said to her : " Do thou offer thy life anew." The possibility of suffering for others is a necessary consequence of the teaching on the Mystical Body given by St. Paul, who could say of himself that he filled up in his body what was lacking in the sufferings of Christ. For the sufferings of the mystics are in a very real sense the extension of the Passion, and the redemptive power accorded to them by Divine Love is part of the great redemptive process, perfectly accomplished by the author of our Redemption on the Cross, yet mystically " filled up " in the sufferings of the members of His Body, which is the Church.

Thus the last months of St. Catherine's life were a slow crucifixion in which she, purified of her own faults as she had doubtless long been, could offer the sufferings of her soul and body in expiation for the Church Militant. Shortly before her death a sign was given her of her approaching end : she felt the ship of the Church resting on her shoulders and fainted under the weight. The last Lent of her life she heard Mass at dawn every day. At the hour of Terce she went to St. Peter's, where she remained in prayer for the peace of the Church till Vespers, thus fulfilling her own words : " When I depart out of this body, I shall truly have consumed and given my life in the Church and for the Church."

Pretiosa est in conspectu Domini mors Sanctorum ejus. St. Catherine's death was the consummation of her mystic life. She had always desired martyrdom, and if the actual outpouring of her blood was denied her, she poured out her life mystically as an acceptable offering. With her body reduced to no more than skin and bones the living flame of love for God and for His Spouse seems to have literally burned her out, until the life of grace, so powerful in her on earth, could unfold into the unending life of glory in heaven.

Blessed Anna Maria Taigi, A Mystic in the Family.

SIENA may be called the city of unusual vocations. There is, as we have just seen, St. Catherine, its greatest daughter, who brought back the Pope from Avignon and was espoused to Our Lord ; there is St. Bernardine, ardent Apostle and lover of the Name of Jesus ; and there is, very near our own time, Bl. Anna Maria Taigi, mother of a large family, mystic and confidante of Popes. She was born in the same year as Napoleon (1769) with whose family she was later brought into close relations. Unlike in this to her great compatriot, she gave no early signs of future sanctity. She was the daughter of an apothecary, a spendthrift who went to Rome with his family when Anna was six. She was sent to a convent school where she learned embroidery, and afterwards her father found her a job as housemaid with a rich lady of doubtful reputation. In her house she spent three years, learning all the secrets of female vanity and becoming conscious of her own attraction for men. It was a perilous position for a poor and pretty young girl, and the dangers were not altogether removed even when, in 1790, she married Domenico Taigi, a valet in the Palazzo Chigi, considerably older than herself. During the first year of her marriage she fully gave herself up to the pleasures of the world ; her husband bought her trinkets and fine dresses and took her to dances and other amusements. It was the time when Europe was shaken by the French Revolution, and soon she began to feel strange scruples about the life of vanity and empty pleasures which she was leading. One day a Servite priest met her, walking in the road with Domenico, and he heard an interior voice saying to him : " Look at this woman. I shall one day entrust her to you. You will convert her because I have chosen her for a Saint."

At the end of the year, soon after the birth of her first child, Anna went to confession to a Servite Father unknown to her and was received with the words : " So you have come at last. Be of good cheer, my child, God loves you, and in return He asks for your whole heart." From that day a new life began for her ; a life lived in the most humdrum circumstances of a numerous family, harassed by crushing work and constant poverty which she met with the most absolute trust in Divine Providence which, indeed, never failed her. Yet this to all appearance quite ordinary life was pervaded through and through by the supernatural life of grace, by grace that is not hindered by material obstacles but rather uses them as the consummate sculptor uses a block of marble, transforming the hard bulk of the stone into a wonder of spiritual beauty.

Here was a chosen soul, not in the cloister protected by rules, reminded of her Creator at all hours of day and night by bells, Office and periods of prayer, but in a small house, with an exacting husband, a cantankerous mother, and an increasing number of children and later also of grandchildren, all depending on her for food, dress, cleanliness and the innumerable requirements of a large household. How is it possible to lead the most exalted mystical life in such circumstances ?

Shortly after her conversion Anna Maria was told by Our Lady that it was her special vocation to show to the world that sanctity can be attained in every walk of life, even without extraordinary bodily penances, but on one condition : the perfect mortification of self-will. It seems that this was precisely the reason why Divine Providence had placed her in a position so apparently unfavourable to the development of the mystic life. She fulfilled the condition to perfection. She served her husband with the utmost humility, obeying him as if he were the Lord Himself, leaving bishops and princesses who came to consult her to undo Domenico's shoes when he came home and to place his dinner on the table. She bore with her gossiping mother who spoiled her children, and nursed her in a repulsive illness without receiving a word of thanks in return ; she supported her father who refused to work, and she brought up her three boys and four girls and kept the peace in a house full of the most violent and divergent temperaments. Where, in this overcrowded life, could there be a place for contemplative prayer ?

Yet mystic graces were showered on her almost from the beginning of her conversion. From that time all through her life she enjoyed an extraordinary gift similar to St. Hildegard's light ; she saw before her a " mystic sun," a brilliant globe of light encircled by a crown of thorns in which she read the future as well as events in distant places with perfect clarity ; but she never used this gift unless charity or obedience demanded it. During the first years of her mystic life ecstasies were frequent : suddenly while she was at table or doing housework, her eyes would close, her limbs grow rigid, and Domenico would angrily shout at her why she must go to sleep in the middle of the day—but there was no answer, and the children began to cry, thinking that their mother was dead. After Holy Communion she was almost always in ecstasy, and Our Lord often appeared to her in the Blessed Sacrament. After she had been received into the Third Order of the Holy Trinity, which she had chosen because of her ardent devotion to this greatest of the Christian mysteries, He revealed to her her special vocation : " Know," He said," that I have chosen you to convert sinners and to console those who suffer in every walk of life, priests and religious and even My Vicar himself. You will meet with falsehood and perfidy, you will be mocked, despised and calumniated, but you will endure it all for love of Me."

The prophecy was soon to be fulfilled. After the joyous spring of her spiritual life, rich with sensible graces, there followed dark years of desolation. She had the most violent temptations to doubt and even to hatred of God, and seemed no longer to know the meaning of love. She appeared to herself completely abandoned by the Divine mercy, feeling as if confined to a corner of hell, though, strangely enough, her supernatural lights never failed her. At the same time she was overwhelmed by exterior trials : priests refused her Holy Communion, neighbours accused her of secret sins, and she was afflicted by mysterious and very painful illnesses. For it seems that God opposed the humble housewife to Napoleon, who imprisoned the Pope and persecuted the Church, as a victim of expiation. She foretold his fall with precise details and knew the most intimate sentiments of the dying Emperor. In 1815 his mother, Madame Letizia, and his brother Cardinal Fesch came to live near her in Rome, and under the influence of Anna, whom they venerated, both became devout. One day, when the Cardinal asked her to pray for the recovery

of his sister she answered with the holy liberty of the Saints :
" Tell her Highness to meditate on these three points : what she
has been, what she is, and what she will be, and at the same time
to prepare herself for death." Yet she was not strong enough
to overcome their longings to revive past greatness, and in 1831
they prepared to dethrone Gregory XVI and to crown Napoleon's
son Emperor of Rome. Anna, who like St. Catherine, endured
agonies for the Church, saw their preparations in her mystic sun,
denounced the plot to the authorities, and paid for the delivery
by untold sufferings. The same happened when the peace of the
Church was threatened by socialism and the machinations of the
Carbonari, in fulfilment of Our Lord's words to her : " I have
chosen you to be counted among my martyrs by an invisible
martyrdom. None will know, none will understand, only I."

The mystery of expiation by suffering as evident in Bl. Anna
Maria's as in St. Catherine's life is a difficulty to many of our
contemporaries. Yet from the time of the martyrs, whose blood
the Fathers called the " seed of the Church," the Church has
always counted on the sufferings of her members to continue the
work of her Head. The faith was spread throughout Europe
by martyrs and confessors, whose journeyings through the forests
and the hostile tribes of Britain and Germany, Poland and
Hungary, must have involved privations hard to imagine
in our time of railways and aeroplanes. And when Europe had
been converted, there was that innate drift to laxity, error and ease
to be exorcised by the long disciplines of a St. Dominic, the Stigmata
of St. Francis and the agonies of St. Catherine, so strangely akin
to those of the modern Beata. For to the mystery of iniquity
there will be always opposed the mystery of suffering, to the Tree
of forbidden Knowledge the Tree of the Cross, to infidelity
self-sacrifice, to the lust and cruelty of the great the pains and
penances of the humble. This is the mysterious and hidden law
of the supernatural world, of which we are sometimes allowed
glimpses in the lives of the Saints, though they are rarely so clear
as in the lives of St. Catherine and Bl. Anna Taigi. Both co-
operated to the full with the designs of Divine Providence, for
Anna, too, never allowed herself any distraction to alleviate her
trials. She understood perfectly Our Lord's words to her which
sound almost as if they came from St. Catherine's *Dialogue* :
" True sanctity consists in bearing patiently interior and exterior

trials. A soul which suffers patiently the tribulations which come to her through the medium of creatures is greater than one who gives herself to works of penance."

Yet, no more than St. Catherine, did she dispense herself from corporal austerities, which all the Saints have embraced as eagerly as the children of this world seek for comfort and riches. Though her husband and children were watching her, she contrived to deprive herself of drink for days and sometimes weeks in the hot Roman summer. She ate extremely little and that mostly standing, while serving the others, and taking for herself the worst pieces. She used disciplines and hairshirts, made pilgrimages barefoot, yet never neglected her domestic duties.

It is by such a life as this, of obedience and self-effacement, that miracles are accomplished. One day, when Anna was ill, Our Lord appeared to her, took her right hand in His and told her to rise. From that time she suffered almost constant pains in that hand, which increased on Fridays, but, in exchange, she had received the gift of healing. With it, she effected innumerable cures, one of the most famous was that of the Queen of Etruria Marie-Louise de Bourbon, whom she healed of epilepsy. She also healed souls, and, again like St. Catherine, she was a great peacemaker, who loved especially to reconcile families. But what likens her perhaps more than anything else to the great Dominican was her relations with the Papacy. She predicted the return of Pius VII from his captivity at Fontainebleau, she was consulted by him and his successors, particularly by Leo XII and Gregory XVI, who asked her advice daily, and she foretold the election of Pius IX when he was still an unknown missionary priest. It was for the Popes that she most willingly offered her sufferings, and Our Lord promised her that while she lived there would be no revolution in Rome.

As her life had been spent in suffering, so her death was preceded by an illness of seven months, during which she was wrecked with asthma and rheumatism, while the medical treatment she received increased rather than alleviated her pains. By a strange combination of circumstances she endured her last agony alone, as she had foretold, though her house was full of priests and relatives. When the cause of her Beatification was introduced there was an extraordinary array of witnesses. For besides Cardinals and priests there were her husband, her children, her daughter-in-law, all testifying that the mystic who had known the highest regions of Divine contemplation and the terrifying depths of the Dark Night, had been an exemplary wife and mother. "I have always found her docile and submissive like a lamb" said Domenico, and "she arranged everything so sweetly that we did what she wanted in spite of ourselves." It is one of the marvels of grace that, while the great ones of the world generally lose in stature when observed too closely, the Saints seem more admirable the more intimately they are known. Yet even in the annals of sanctity it is a rare case that perfection should be recognized by a hot-tempered husband and a domineering daughter-in-law. It is a triumph of love—for the mystic life is nothing else but the full flowering of charity—a charity that beareth all things, believeth all things, hopeth all things and endureth all things, and is finally made perfect in the Beatific Vision where both faith and hope are left behind.

CHAPTER II

A Dominican Trio

Master Eckhart

THE fourteenth century was a period particularly fertile in mysticism : there were, to mention only a few names, St. Catherine of Siena and Ruysbroeck, the English mystics Mother Julian and the author of the *Cloud of Unknowing*, and there is the great Dominican triad, Master Eckhart, Tauler and Suso. Strangely enough, though belonging to the same Order, they represent three very different kinds of mysticism. Master Eckhart is the speculative mystic, the philosopher, Tauler the practical mystic, the preacher, and Suso is the affectionate type, the lover ; and both Tauler and Suso are devoted disciples of Master Eckhart.

Little is known of Eckhart's outer life. Born somewhere in Thuringia about 1260, he probably entered the Dominican convent at Erfurt as a youth. His great intellectual gifts were soon recognised, for he was sent to Paris to complete his education at the fount of medieval scholarship. On his return to Germany he was elected Provincial of his Order. As such he was entrusted with the supervision of all Dominican convents in Northern Germany, and, after some time, with the reform of the houses in the Bohemian Province as well. About 1310 he was relieved of these administrative duties, and again sent to Paris as teacher of his Order. Three years later he returned to Germany, living first at Strasbourg and afterwards at Cologne, where he became one of the most influential preachers. As, at that time, one of the chief duties of the Dominicans was the spiritual direction of communities of religious women, Master Eckhart's sermons were mostly addressed to them. In these communities an exuberant inner life had sprung up, and Eckhart, reared in the intellectual discipline of St. Thomas, brought his great learning to the task of weaning the devout women from undue attachment to visions and other striking experiences and to lead them to the purity of mystic contemplation.

But in these heights human language becomes sadly inadequate. It was Master Eckhart's tragedy that he tried to express the inexpressible, and in doing so had to use paradoxical statements that savoured of false doctrine. So the last years of his life were overshadowed by a trial for heresy, which eventually led to the condemnation of twenty-six of his theses, though most of these were admitted to be susceptible of an orthodox interpretation.

" In my sermons," Master Eckhart once said, " I usually speak of four things. Firstly of abandonment, and that man should get rid of himself and of all things. Secondly that we should again be formed into the one good, which is God. Thirdly that we should all remember the noble quality which God has laid in the soul, through which man is meant to enter into the marvellous life of God. Fourthly I speak of the purity of the Divine Nature."

This ascending scale which begins with the creature and ends with the Creator is, as it were, the structure which supports the edifice of Master Eckhart's doctrine.

If man would then ascend into these heights the first thing Eckhart bids him do is to go out from himself. It is not enough that he should leave the good things of this world, this is only the indispensable preparation. For abandonment, the foundation of Eckhart's mystic spire, means poverty of spirit, the complete giving up of one's own will. If the soul is to know God she must lose herself, accepting with joyful gratitude whatever God may lay upon her, even though it be nothing but ignominy, pain and sorrow, and living untouched by emotions, " as though she were dead." Yet this detachment from self is not Stoic insensibility. " No Saint is too great to be moved," said Master Eckhart, and again, with a touch of dry humour that is characteristic of him : " I could never reach a stage where an unpleasant noise would sound as lovely to my ears as string-music."

But is not this frank admission of normal reactions incompatible with the stern demand that man should be " altogether dead " to natural inclinations ? Eckhart himself provided the solution of the difficulty by placing " detachment " not in human sensibility, but in the will. " This," he says, "we should attain : that a true will, formed by God, free itself from all natural desires. If then wise insight would see occasion to order the will to turn away, that will should speak : I do it willingly." The Thomist hierarchy within the human being is observed : reason commands and the will obeys.

In the stress on the interplay of reason, will, and the other human faculties and instincts lies the key to Eckhart's so-called " dialectical " mode of thinking, which has often so puzzled his interpreters that they do not know whether to call him a quietist or an activist, a Theist or a Pantheist. But he cannot be thus conveniently labelled, for the simple reason that he sees man as he is, a being between heaven and earth, with reason to govern his instincts, yet subject to them through sin. Thus he has to live in constant tension ; yet as will and instincts are more and more trained to follow the superior faculty of the soul, the inner man becomes increasingly detached from self, resting in that peace that surpasses all understanding.

It is at this stage, when she has emptied herself of the world and of self, that the soul climbs higher, and begins to be " informed " into God. When God finds her perfectly detached He cannot but attach Himself to her. This work of union which God performs in the soul is entirely a work of His grace. Seeing that she has given up everything for His sake, He " lifts up our humanity above all that belongs to us as creatures, and brings it higher than the nature of all angels into the unity where God and man are One." This is the true end of man, this is the purpose of the Incarnation, this the joy and glory of creation, that man be " converted " into God, that the Son of God be born in his soul, that the creature be perfectly united to Him who created it.

This " Birth of the Son " in the soul is one of Master Eckhart's most characteristic conceptions. It is the most hidden work that God performs in the depth of man's nature. " In this hour of birth," says Eckhart," the soul refuses everything that is not God, for God leads His bride away from all creatures into Himself. . . . In this my eternal birth I am born from eternity, and shall abide eternally." For in this new birth God and the soul become One : " God in His grace has made the soul like unto Himself."

Master Eckhart here uses bold language, indeed, raising man to a height from whence even wars and the rumours of wars seem insignificant. Timid souls have asked themselves whether this can still be called Christianity, and audacious ones deny it, only to proclaim that Master Eckhart is the founder of a higher, pantheistic " German " religion. But when the Dominican author of a Commentary on the Fourth Gospel preached on the Mystic Union in words that seemed almost to annihilate the frontier between God and man he but followed his Master who had once prayed :

"For them also (do I pray) that shall believe in me. . . . that they all may be one ; as thou, Father, in me, and I in thee, that they also may be one in us . . . and the glory which thou hast given me I have given to them ; that they may be one, as we also are one ; I in them, and thou in me, that they may be perfected into one." (John 17. 20 ff.)

It is no less than unity between God and man for which St. John's Incarnate Logos prayed in His High-priestly Prayer, ringing the changes on the tremendous word " One." Eckhart, the metaphysician of the *Unio Mystica*, takes up the theme ; for it is his most assured conviction that God has made man and was Himself made Man in the person of the Son, in order that man might become One with Him.

Eckhart never tells us whether he himself has experienced this highest state of union. He, like his master St. Thomas, belongs to those rare religious personalities who keep an almost unbroken silence on their own spiritual life. It matters nothing whether this particular " Brother Eckhart " has been vouchsafed the grace of the mystic union—what alone concerns him is that man should come to know his own soul and her relationship to his Maker.

Thus, with the utmost care and yet with the glowing passion of a soul freed from all earthly desires, Eckhart, in his doctrine of the human soul, raises the next arch of his mystic spire to still greater heights. When man has once grasped what union with God means his own soul becomes a mystery to him, and he asks with the Psalmist : " What is man that thou art mindful of him, and the son of man that thou visitest him ? " Where, in the intricate structure of the human being, is the point at which he is capable of God, *capax Dei* as St. Augustine calls it ?

"What the soul is in her ground, " answers Eckhart, " no man can know. What we may know about her is supernatural, and this knowledge can be caused only by grace. There works the mercy of God." Here we have left the realm of philosophical speculation and are in the sphere of Revelation, where every statement should be prefaced : " By the grace of God." For Master Eckhart is a true disciple of St. Thomas, the great theologian of grace, and more jealous of the glory of God than of the honour of man—but man is by grace a child of God and destined for union with Him, therefore no words seem too strong to express his ineffable dignity. For whatever he will have to say about the grandeur of the human soul, this grandeur is not an achievement of man, but the free gift of God.

"What the soul is in her ground. . . ." That is the centre of Master Eckhart's teaching. The ground of the soul, *Scintilla animae*, is the Divine principle in man, the source of reason and love, though higher than either of these, so that neither reason nor love can know it, since the higher cannot be known by the lower. *Scintilla*, the "spark," is that quality in the soul which points always to God as the magnetic needle points north. It is so closely related to, yet so decidedly different from, Him, that Eckhart can express this extraordinary relationship only by a paradox : "God is the soul—and yet He is not the soul."

It is Eckhart's peculiar greatness, but at the same time also his danger, that he had the courage to leave this contradiction as it stands without solving, and thereby dissolving it. "God is the soul—yet God is not the soul" ; this indeed defies what Cardinal Newman called "paper-logic." For it is expressive of the highest logic of the living relationship between God and His creature. God, in His grace, has raised the soul to such a degree of likeness with Himself that human language breaks in the attempt to define it. Divine Revelation itself hints at the mystery by calling man created *ad imaginem Dei*. Master Eckhart's "ground of the soul" is nothing but a paraphrase of this *ad imaginem*, Divine yet not God, created yet reflecting the uncreated Deity. "This," he says, "is a natural image of God, which God has impressed upon every soul. I cannot say more, else it would be God Himself and this it is not, or God would not be God."

For he never loses consciousness of the essential difference between God and the soul. He may exalt the "spark" to the closest kinship with God, yet always with the tacit presupposition that what belongs to God by nature belongs to the soul only by grace. Thus the soul depends upon God for her very God-likeness, and the more she receives the more dependent she becomes. He, therefore, who has penetrated into his own "ground" and knows himself to be "God, yet not God" will bear this knowledge with the deepest humility. For above the soul, moulded in the image of God, is He Who made her, for whom she is for ever longing.

He, however, as Eckhart well knew, "never reveals Himself completely in this life, so that even His revelation is as nothing compared with what He really is."

Eckhart was, of course, perfectly familiar with St. Thomas's teaching on God. With a disciple's reverence he follows the crystal-clear thought of the *Summa* : God is absolute Being and Immutable Perfection, Being and Intelligence are one in Him, to Him alone belong perfect Unity and Simplicity. He only is good. All this is true of God—and yet, is it really the whole truth ? Are our little conceptions of Being, Perfection, Goodness, applicable to God, who is above even our most exalted thought of Him ? Is there no other way of expressing His transcendence ? Centuries before Eckhart the same question had confronted that mystic thinker well known to St. Thomas and the other Scholastic theologians, whose works have come down to us under the name of Dionysius Areopagita. His answer to the problem was the *Via Negativa*, i.e., the definition of God by negations. Thus, when Master Eckhart had exhausted the Thomist affirmations without finding full satisfaction in them, he turned to Dionysius for his passionate negatives.

" No tongue," Eckhart says, "can devise a word to define God, because of the highness and clarity of His being. God is the No of God, the No of Spirit, the No of Person, the No of every image." He even goes so far as to say that God is not Being, not Goodness but he immediately adds : " In denying Him this, I have not denied Him Being, but exalted it." For all these negatives, piled one upon the other in his insatiable thirst for expression, are not meant to take anything away from God, but to increase the majesty of His transcendence. They flow from the humility of the creature that knows that whatever words it may use, they can but touch the hem of the garment of the incomprehensible Godhead.

Yet despite this humility Eckhart is too great a thinker to end with negation. In a last magnificent effort to grasp what, by its very nature, must for ever elude human thought, he dares to do once more what he did before, in his teaching on the soul. Side by side, without any attempt at reconciliation, he places thesis and antithesis : " God is wroth without wrath, extensive without extension, good without quality—always one and the other of two contradictions." God is all these dialectical opposites, yet

He is one, is indeed so much One that man cannot even form a conception of this One-ness.

This is the last tension to which his dialectical thinking leads Master Eckhart on his mystic way. Beyond that, " What is the last end ? " he asks. " It is the hiddenness of the darkness of the eternal Godhead, and is unknown, and has never been made known and will never be known."

The mystic spire has at last reached the cloud of Divine Darkness, the " Cloud of Unknowing "—or is it Divine Light ? Here human eyes can no longer distinguish between Darkness and Light, but the cloud is the same that overshadowed the Tabernacle of the Israelites in the wilderness, and that hid the glorified and ascending Christ from His disciples.

But it is a perilous task to build as high as the clouds. Master Eckhart's daring dialectic, preached to congregations of un-lettered women, might, indeed, lead a chosen few into the highway of contemplation, but how should ordinary souls understand his passionate antitheses ? He himself was aware of the peril, for more than once he told his hearers not to be troubled if they did not understand his meaning. The Church, however, commanded by her Master not to " offend one of these little ones," condemned what sounded most dangerous in his teaching.

For dangerous it undoubtedly was, and only too easily misunder-stood. One glance at the subsequent history of Master Eckhart's thought will afford sufficient proof. For not only has he been invoked as the forerunner of Luther's Reformation, but also as the father of Kant's Critical Idealism, of Hegelian Pantheism, and, lastly, as ancestor of the Nazi *Deutschreligion*.

Yet he is none of these. Born into a world full of strife and unrest, his soul found the way out of selfhood into her real self, where man, made in the image of God, is caught up into the life of the Godhead. From this hidden centre he lived a life as active and as suffering as any human life must be, in the sure knowledge that the insoluble antinomies, the Yes and No of all earthbound thought, have their solution in the Mind that is the Cause both of them and of those who are for ever trying to solve them. Nor was his work doomed to failure ; it lived on in his disciples and in the mystic life he had fostered in so many souls, and especially among his own brethren, who kept alive the flame he had spent his life to kindle.

D

John Tauler

ONE of Eckhart's most devoted disciples was John Tauler. Unlike his master, he was not an original thinker, but first and foremost a preacher and shepherd of souls. Like St. John the Baptist he was a voice crying in the wilderness of the world : " Repent ye, abandon the creatures and turn to the Creator." This was his battle cry, and his life work was to show man how to fulfil its demand. Whereas Suso made his own life a mirror, as it were, of the mystic way, reflecting in it both its glories and its agonies, Tauler took man by the hand and led him step by step into the Sanctuary of the Mystic Union.

He was eminently fitted for this work, for he had that deep insight into human nature which is indispensable in the preacher and teacher. " Man," he said, " hangs between heaven and earth. With his highest faculties he is exalted above himself and above all things, and dwells in God, but with his lowest faculties he is subjected under all things, into the very ground of humility. He calls the higher faculties the " inner man," whilst the lower faculties form the " outer man." The inner man is subject to God alone, but the outer man to all creatures in true humility. The task of the inner man is of a double nature : he directs the outer man by the light of his superior knowledge, whilst in himself he remains unruffled by the changes of earthly existence, " sunk and united " in his communion with God. The outer man, on the other hand, must await the orders of the inner man. "We must force the outer man," says Tauler, "as far as we can and draw him into the other man of inwardness. This is the rational man, and it means that the outer man is to work and walk according to the order of the rational man, and not according to his own animal desires."

In this psychology Tauler's mystical doctrine is firmly rooted, and we have not far to go to discover its origin. It is the teaching of his master St. Thomas, who saw man as a rational being whose faculties are well ordered. Like Eckhart, he insists on the hierarchical structure of human nature : reason, which knows God to be the absolute Good, imparts the right direction to the will, which in its turn rules the affections. This is the ground from which all else springs ; without this Thomist psychology the mystic way

which Tauler does not weary to describe would remain unintelligible.

It is the more important to keep this in mind, as few thinkers
have been so consistently misrepresented as the fourteenth century
German mystics. It has been their misfortune to have been
re-discovered by Protestant professors of literature in the nineteenth century. Misled by Luther's early admiration for Tauler
and Master Eckhart, these scholars who had no knowledge of
Thomist theology regarded those Dominicans as virtual pre-
decessors of the Reformation, thinking that they proclaimed a
peculiarly " German " and " interior " piety as opposed to the
" outward ceremonial " of " Roman " Catholicism. Even the
painstaking researches of Catholic scholars like Denifle and Karrer
(though taken into account by some Protestant theologians such
as Harnack) cannot be said to have succeeded in rectifying the
ideas of more than a few experts.

Yet the mysticism of the fourteenth-century German Dominicans
is Thomist in its essence. Their system is built upon the similitude
between Creator and creature, which is, indeed, marred by sin,
but by the grace of God can be recovered by purgation and
illumination. This conception is diametrically opposed to the
Lutheran dogma of the total depravity of human nature and to
" justification by faith." It is, on the contrary, built on the Angelic
Doctor's teaching that grace does not destroy, but restores and
perfects nature, since the image of God in which man is made
was never altogether annihilated. This image of God that is to
be restored in man is called by Tauler the " third man " ; for
when the rational man has completely subdued the outer man,
the inner man can " turn into his origin where he has been from
all eternity."

The indispensable condition of becoming a wholly spiritual
man is humility, a virtue that plays so important a part in Tauler's
teaching that it is sometimes called the " mysticism of humility."
"We must all humble ourselves. This is the foundation on which
all man's life and work is to be built—or else all will break down.
For God seeks and wants a humble man." Here speaks the preacher
and guide of souls, who knows the ravages that spiritual pride
can cause in them, especially in those vowed by their profession
to a life of perfection. It is, to him, the worst of all vices, and it
may well have been that he saw its disastrous consequences in

some of the convents where he used to preach ; for he frequently
warns his hearers that their habit will not save them if their inner
man be not in the right state of meekness.

Even the humble man, however, who is setting out on the way
of mystic perfection, is still confined in five " prisons " from
which he must strive to be freed. Love of creatures and love of
self prevent him from loving his Creator as he ought. Reason,
which tries to solve all difficulties by its own power, bars the
entrance of faith. Here again we have not the forerunner of
Luther's scorn of human reason and of his peculiar theology or
faith, but the follower of St. Thomas, who was so anxious to
define and keep intact the border line between faith and reason.
The third prison, especially dangerous in communities of women,
is undue reliance on sensible devotion and visionary experiences.
Tauler is never tired of denouncing them as an end in themselves,
though he admits their relative value as helps on the way to the
Mystic Union. In this he is in line with all great mystics, especially
with St. John of the Cross, and he adduces the same reasons as
the Carmelite. For man can easily be deceived, and more often
than not feelings of devotion and visions may be caused by his
—or her—own imagination or even by the devil rather than
by the action of Almighty God.

Yet when the soul has been delivered from all these prisons
there is still one left, the most subtle of all. It is the roots of self-
will ; for even when a man has generously turned from creatures
and sensible satisfactions to the love of God alone, there will
still be vestiges of self-will and a desire of God's grace from selfish
interests. This, too, must go. Should it be God's will to refuse
grace man must conform to this will and resign himself without
despairing to a state outside His grace, thus fulfilling the Divine
Will. It must be admitted that, if taken literally, this sounds like
a flat contradiction of the theological axiom : *Facienti quod in se
est Deus non denegat gratiam,* and like an anticipation of Quietism.
But viewed in connection with the whole of Tauler's teaching
it ought not to be condemned as savouring of heresy. The stress
he lays throughout his preaching on definite acts of love, praise
and charity, excludes this. We have here the phenomenon of
quasi-heretical statements *prout sonant* which is so often found in
mystical teaching, and more especially in the Northern mystics,
whose thought and language are far less precise than those of the

Latins, though even a St. Francis de Sales sometimes uses similar terms. All that is meant by such exaggerated expressions is that the mystic must abandon himself entirely to God's adorable will, letting Him do with him whatever He pleases.

However exalted his speculative teaching on abandonment, Tauler is eminently practical when he comes to give advice on how it is to be achieved. His restraint in this matter is probably due to the sound balance of the Thomist system in which he was reared. For Thomism, in contrast to all Manichean heresies, treats man as the intermediate being he is, respecting his body no less than his soul. At a time, therefore, when religious excitement was apt to run to wild excesses of asceticism on the one hand and to libertinism on the other, as in the cases of the Flagellants, and of the "Brethren of the Free Spirit" respectively, the Dominican mystics exercised a wholesome restraint. With a Thomist respect for the differences among men, each of whom is a person in his own right, an individual substance rational by nature, Tauler pointed out that the way to God cannot be the same for each one of us. The peace of Christ is, indeed, achieved only by suffering and self-denial ; but every man must take account of his own personal needs. His views on ascetic practices sound surprisingly modern and not at all like what many of us would expect from a medieval director. For he points out that, while fasting and vigils will help some to prepare themselves for union with God, others may only find their health undermined by them without having drawn any nearer to Christ. In harmony with the emphasis his Order lays on the need for personal responsibility, he tells his hearers that man has to find out for himself what will best lead him to "abandonment" ; and, once this state of the soul is reached, he will set out on the Mystic Way which will lead him to perfect union.

The beginning of this way of prayer will again be different for different temperaments ; from the vast treasure house of Christian devotion every soul must choose what she finds most helpful. "Take for yourself," he says, "what you think will draw you nearest to God : the Life of Christ, or the Passion, or the Wounds of Love, or the Divine Nature or the Blessed Trinity—whatever may draw you most, that take and sink with it into the ground and await God with gratitude." At this initial stage the affections play a great part in Tauler's teaching ; they create, as it were, a favourable atmosphere for the Union between Creator and creature. In accordance with the popular devotion of the time he considered the contemplation of the Five Wounds as particularly helpful, following the sound medieval principle : *Per Christum hominem ad Christum Deum.* His language vibrates with his own love for them ; " The wounds of Our Lord," he says, "are all salvation ; let the holy five wounds remain open until the Last Day . . . these five doors shall be our inheritance here, through which we shall enter into the eternal inheritance of our Father's Kingdom. Through these wounds of love let us learn five lessons : how to abandon and how to suffer, how to be silent and how to despise the world, and lastly how to deny ourselves in true detachment." For his ascetical doctrine is intimately bound up with his teaching on prayer. The consideration of the mysteries of Christ is never an isolated exercise of reason or imagination, but must immediately touch the will : consideration of Our Lord's abandonment must produce abandonment in us, His suffering will teach us how to suffer, His silence will produce the silence in our souls which will lead us to contemplation, and His detachment from the world and from the desires of His own human nature will teach us to overcome the world and ourselves.

Thus meditation on the Life and Passion of Christ will open up for man the mystic way, which Tauler describes with an insight into the progress of the soul which places him in the ranks of the great masters of the spiritual life. The first stage, after man has turned to God by penance and meditation, is one of unspeakable joy. The soul " drinks in God with all her might, so that she becomes inebriated with Him and completely forgets herself. Then she would gladly go through fire and water and a thousand swords." This exultant state Tauler calls *jubilacio.* It is the characteristic of the beginnings of the mystic life and may perhaps correspond to the state of joy and delight described by St. Teresa in the prayer of loving recollection and of Quiet, though these identifications are always uncertain, as the medieval mystics are far less precise in their classifications than their post-Tridentine brethren. When the joy of the soul has reached this climax where she has been allowed to taste and see that the Lord is sweet, she is suddenly cast down from the heights of her happiness, for she is not yet strong enough to soar higher, and presently falls into a deep despondency. This is the second stage of the way, compared to the state of Job when "the spirit went from him." Man must now pass through what St. John of the Cross calls the "Dark Night of the Soul," probably the second night, the "Night of the Spirit," that prepares for perfect union. Now the soul is tossed about like a ball between knowledge and ignorance, certainty and uncertainty, tranquillity and unrest, confidence and fear. It is the unsettled state of the man who has left the human mode of living and is introduced to the Divine life, for which these painful purgings prepare him. What is the poor soul to do in these exhausting struggles ? Tauler answers that through all these she shall pass in faith, hope and humility, and not despair, for "those who must suffer in this dark misery will become the most lovable and noble of men. But nature must die many a death." Nature, that is all the selfish and sinful instincts of man must die, so that grace may unfold unhindered, for "he who loses his life for My sake shall find it." This is the burden of all mystic teaching, that we must die in order to live, as it is the teaching of Our Lord Himself, who is the source of all Christian mysticism.

For it is only in the school of suffering that the last stains of self-will are purged and the soul is made ready for the ultimate stages of the Mystic Way, for ecstasy and the transforming union, though Tauler does not use these technical terms of a later age. In this state "the human spirit is drawn high above its powers into a wild desert of which no man can speak, into the hidden darkness of God." In this Union is born the kindling of the fire of love, "then there is a mist, a darkness, in which your spirit is stolen away for about half an *Ave Maria*, so that you are beside your senses and your natural reason. And in this darkness God speaks to you in truth." There are all the elements of ecstasy, which the medieval Dominican describes in much the same way as St. Teresa three hundred years later. It is true, he gives a much shorter duration to the actual rapture than the Carmelite, who assigns to it about half an hour. But these details must necessarily vary considerably, as they depend on so many factors, both super-natural and psychological. This mystic union, in which perfect love is born, is the true end of man here on earth, and, like all the great mystics, Tauler ardently desires that all men should attain to it. Therefore, he preaches the mystic life in season and out of season.

One almost hears the voice of the preacher, promising, enticing, even cajoling his hearers to leave the pleasures of the " Lady World " for a higher and more lasting satisfaction : " Then there is a feast," he says, " and the kitchen smells so sweetly of all the good dishes prepared therein.   Then May is in its full bloom ; for a single drop of the delights which the Holy Ghost prepares exceeds and extinguishes all the taste and sweetness that all creatures can produce."

Yet it is not for this momentary sweetness that the Mystic Union should be desired, but for its effects on the soul.   Its most precious fruit is the right ordering of all the faculties of man.   After the exultation of the moment of actual union is passed, " man shall do much more than he did before ; he shall love more, thank more, praise more, and live more deeply than before."   For though the soul be perfectly passive in the actual state of union, God's action is such that she is filled with Divine energy which manifests itself in the increase of virtue throughout man's ordinary life.   To the Christian mystic, therefore, the *Unio mystica* is not to be desired as a permanent state to which all else is subjected—this would be the Quietist ideal.   On the contrary, it is a well from which the soul renews not only her own strength for the battle of life, but with whose limpid waters she will also refresh others.   *Contemplata aliis tradere*—this vocation, which St. Thomas considers to be the highest, Tauler fulfilled in his own life and in his work for souls. Thus the indefatigable preacher of the true life of the spirit in an age of discord and lukewarmness had a right to hold in his hand the Book of Life, as his tombstone shows him, and to have engraved on his breast the Holy Name IHS and underneath the T, which stands both for his initial and for the burden of his preaching, the Cross.

Blessed Henry Suso.

You must not think that you shall take leave from love.   Behold, they who said they loved you could not love.   And if your heart were as full of love as the bottomless sea, it would all be drunk in by the love of the Beautiful Lover.

HENRY SUSO.

THE Cross that was the burden of Tauler's preaching, was the very essence of Suso's life, the most gentle and the most attractive of the Dominican Trio.   In him the influence of the highly strung

spirituality of the nuns under his direction and the theological
austerity of his Dominican training produced a wonderfully
enriched mystic life. Securely rooted in Thomist doctrine, the
flower of Dominican mysticism drew from the Angelic Doctor
all his learning, sanity and balance, developing its own mystic
elements in the less restrained atmosphere of feminine tenderness
and devotion.

In the case of Suso, this combination of sound theology and
spiritual sensibility took root in the temperament of a poet and
artist, bringing forth fruits of particular loveliness. His very life
seems to be a cycle of poems or a series of delicate miniatures
painted on the gold ground of a deep faith in God and His Church.
And as in the case of every real artist nothing but his heart-blood
can give his work its finish, so in Henry Suso's life, this spiritual
work of art, suffering " even unto blood " was needed for its
perfection.

" There was a preacher in Germany, a Swabian by birth, whose
name be written in the book of life. This man desired to become
and be called a servant of Eternal Wisdom." Thus opens Suso's
autobiography, and to complete his self-description he adds simply:
" He had, from his youth, a heart full of love." All his writings
breathe this love ; but he soon learned that " suffering, by old
right, belongs to love," and willingly accepted both as the foundation of his spiritual knighthood. For there is perhaps no term
more expressive of his mystic life than that of the Knight-Errant
or Minnesinger. Of noble birth, he had inherited the ideals of
medieval chivalry so intimately connected with the Christian life
of his time, and he transferred them quite naturally, or shall we
rather say supernaturally, from the court to the cloister. He
consecrated himself to the service of Christ, the Eternal Wisdom,
in much the same way as a knight devoted his life to the service
of his lady. But instead of fighting tournaments and battles in
her honour, the Dominican friar wrestled against flesh and blood,
against principalities and powers, subduing his body by a relentless
asceticism. He held that if the knights of this world are willing
to suffer so much for the small reward earthly love can bestow,
much more should men be willing to suffer for the eternal prize
that Divine Love will give them. Suso was keenly aware of the
difficulties besetting the soul on her way to mystic union. " The
mount is high," he wrote, " and the way slippery ; it cannot be

gained in a moment, it means trying again and again until it be conquered." And the first task he set himself in the service of his Divine Master was to conquer the love of this world in his own passionate heart.

Perhaps the most painful renunciation was the first : the breaking away from all his friends and from the sympathy they could give him. This separation, so bitter yet so essential to the contemplative life, as the experience of St. Teresa clearly shows, cost his sensitive nature more than we might gather from his shy admission: " Therefore he walked miserable and without love." This rejection of human society, however, was only the beginning of a life of the most vigorous ascetic discipline. " The dusk of the senses is the dawn of truth," for " so long as one drop of blood is still unmortified and unconquered, so long art thou lacking." St. John of the Cross himself did not preach a more austere doctrine —but then he, too, was a poet, and, it may be, that to a poetic nature mortification is even more necessary than to others, less abundantly gifted, because there has to be a more thorough purification of the sensibility.

He showed, indeed, from the first that he was both a poet expressing his love in symbols, and a lover filling these symbols with the fire of his passion. To remind himself continually of Him to Whom his young life was consecrated (he was eighteen when he began his ascetic practices) he cut the holy name IHS into the skin above his heart, so that the blood ran down his body " as a sign of love." He was far from contenting himself with the normal ascetic practices. He increased their pain while filling them with symbolic meaning, and displayed the ingenuity of the artist in devising ever new tortures for his body. He scorned the mere hair shirt, and wore iron nails inside it, and round his waist an iron chain, which he did not take off even when he slept. For eight years he bore a wooden cross on his bare back with sharp nails in it, and at least twice a day he " took a discipline with it," as he calls it, hammering the nails into his flesh with his fists. At another time he would sleep with his arms outstretched in the form of a cross, held in position by a complicated mechanism which he had invented, and gave it up only when his hands began to tremble so violently that he was in danger of losing their use altogether. Once he went without drink until his lips were parched and his tongue swollen ; and during two cold German winters he kept a vow not to go near a fire until he could hardly walk for chilblains and ulcers. These things he practised until "his nature was devastated," and he had either to leave off or die. He was told in a vision to give up these exterior mortifications, since all he had done so far was only "a good beginning."

These terrifying self-inflicted pains may perhaps seem abnormal to us, and we shall be unable to comprehend their meaning unless we realise that they are the follies of a lover. The mystic contemplates the Godman stretched out in torments on the Cross, and in his burning desire to give Him love for Love he tortures himself to show forth this love and to have something to give that costs him dear, to say not only in words but in deeds "I love You." It is this fire burning within them that produces these exaggerated penances, and hearts not aglow with it are perhaps shocked by them. But then the Cross, too, shocked both Jews and Greeks, and perhaps it might even shock many Christians to-day if they were not so used to the symbol that it has lost almost all its meaning. To Suso the Cross was the supreme reality, and the sufferings he inflicted on himself were but the means to lead him to the goal of mystic union with the Crucified. "All else," he said, "be it poverty, fasting, watching, and all other mortifications thou shalt direct to this end, and have as many of them as may bring you thither." And when one of his spiritual daughters tried to imitate him in these ascetic practices he reminded her that Christ did not say "take *my* Cross upon you," but "*your* Cross."

In this blood-soaked ground of self-inflicted martyrdom Suso's inner life began to spring up and bear blossom and fruit. *Per Christum Hominem ad Christum Deum* was the *Via Regia* which the disciple of St. Thomas meant to travel to the land of his heart's desire. Two landmarks stand out on this way, guiding the wanderer, the two great subjects of Christian art and devotion ; the Crucifix and the Madonna.

"Lord, mine eyes gaze upon thy dying face, my soul kisses thy fresh wounds full of blood, all my senses are nourished by the sweet fruit under this living tree of the Cross. All my consolation, all my hope, lies for ever in thy Passion." His was no easy, morbid revelling in blood and wounds. He even confessed that he found this contemplation of the Passion very difficult at first. "I sought the Godhead, and found the manhood. I desired sweetness, and found bitterness." For the Eternal Wisdom Himself spoke thus to him : " No man may come to Divine heights of contemplation and sweetness unless he be first drawn by the picture of my human bitterness. My humanity is the way by which man must go, my Passion is the gate through which he must pass who would come to the goal thou seekest. . . . . In my open side thou shalt be lovingly united to my wounded Heart, and there shalt thou make thy abode." *Intra vulnera tua absconde me*, this eternal mystic prayer was lived by Suso, one of the earliest lovers of the Sacred Heart, in its perfection. For all the powers of his soul, his imagination, his intellect and his will he threw into this task of living through the Passion. As his master St. Thomas had set out the sufferings of the Sacred Humanity one by one in the austere Latin of his *Summa*, so Suso tried to reproduce in himself all the bitter sorrow felt by Our Lord and His Mother at every minute of the *Via Crucis* and on Golgotha, until at last he prays to the *Mater Dolorosa* : " Now I desire that thou layest the dead form of thy tender child on the knees of my soul, that I may obtain in spiritual contemplation what thou didst hold in the body."

But when he had filled his soul to overflowing with the sorrowful mysteries of the Passion, he turned to that other mystery : *Vita, dulcedo, et spes nostra.* " Now behold her," he addresses the Christ Child, "now see those dear eyes that often so lovingly looked upon thee, the beautiful cheeks which she so often pressed to thy childish face. Oh, behold those sweet lips which so often tenderly kissed thee, the pure hands that worked in thy service." In the childlike simplicity that is so characteristic of him he went out to gather the first spring flowers and laid them at Our Lady's feet. On the first of May, when the young men used to bring flowers to their girls, he made a crown of roses to put on the Virgin's head, and heard the angels sing hymns in Her honour. To him, as to that other Dominican Saint, St. Catherine of Siena, the most commonplace actions became symbols of heavenly truth : so when he divided an apple into four parts he would eat three in the name of the Holy Trinity and the fourth in the love of the Blessed Virgin. For to him Heaven was a reality come down into his everyday life and he lived with Our Lord and the Saints as naturally as if they were walking with him on earth. His heart was indeed wholly given to his Divine Love, as he himself describes it in an entrancing vision : " And behold, his body above his heart became as pure as crystal, and he saw the Eternal Wisdom sitting quietly in his heart in a beautiful likeness, and with him was sitting the soul of the servant in heavenly desire. And she was bent on his side, and encircled in his arms, and pressed to his divine heart." So vivid was the impression made on him by this vision of union that he made a drawing of it which, though not an artistic masterpiece, yet in its simplicity and holiness reminds one of Fra Angelico.

But he had to pay the price for this close relationship with the Eternal Wisdom, treading the way that his Lord showed him : " Suffering makes man lovable to me, for the suffering man is like unto me. Suffering is the surest way, it is the shortest and the nearest way. It mortifies the body, which must rot away, but nourishes the noble soul, which lives eternally. Suffering draws and forces man to God." Again we are reminded of St. John of the Cross and of the short and steep ascent to Mount Carmel, which is the way of perfect abnegation. Suso, too, was led by this way. When his twenty years of ascetic discipline were over, God took him into His own school, and all self-inflicted torture seemed as nothing before the trials that now awaited him. He was still " like a frightened young hare lying hidden in a bush, afraid of every falling leaf." And to continue his charming simile which shows his almost Franciscan love of nature, the leaves were falling thick and fast indeed. He was exiled from his home because, in the struggle between the Pope and the Emperor, he took the side of the Pope ; he was accused of heresy ; some knights whose daughters and mistresses he had induced to take the veil sought to murder him ; his sister, who was a nun, escaped from her convent and fell into sin ; and, worst of all, one of his penitents, a woman of loose living, who had feigned a conversion in order to obtain material help from the Church, accused him of being the father of her child when he had discovered her deception. This slander was widely believed even by those who had formerly revered him for his sanctity, and though he had no difficulty in disproving it, it took several years to re-establish his reputation. To this sordid tale we owe one of the most touching episodes described in his *Vita*. When the excitement about the slanderous accusation was at its height a woman came to Suso offering to kill the child. Filled with horror at this abominable suggestion, Suso rebuked her vehemently, and then had the child brought to him. He took it on his knees, and when it smiled at him innocently he burst into tears and promised to care for it if nobody else would :

" Oh, you tender child, what a poor little orphan you are. But I will have you as given me by God, and you shall be my dear little child." Then the child, too, began to cry, and " so they wept both together."

It was through these trials borne with all the serenity of which his passionate nature was capable that Suso's mystic life was brought to its perfection. " All the time," he tells us in his autobiography, "while I was only talking about abandonment, I found it sweet to speak of. But now my inmost heart is wounded, and my bone and brain are pierced to the marrow. How then can I be calm ? " Here comes to light what is perhaps one of the deepest differences between Christian mysticism and such doubtful growths as Quietism and other more or less pantheistic systems. The Christian, indeed, demands and seeks detachment from creatures, but to him this does not mean Stoic indifference. " Abandonment," this great watchword of the Dominican mystics, is not the same as insensibility. On the contrary, to feel the pain to the utmost and yet to submit to it is the Christian way, since it was the way of Christ. For Suso, therefore, " a perfect life means giving up one's own will unto the will of God, whether it be bitter or sweet, in subjection and humble obedience."

And so through suffering love is made perfect. Here again Suso takes up the tradition of the knight and minnesinger. For, perhaps, no other time knew so much of the deep connection between love and suffering as the Middle Ages. All the great secular poems, *Tristan*, *Lohengrin*, the *Niblungen*, sing of love that must end in suffering. Only to the friar suffering was not the end, but the way. It was not the dreaded outcome of inevitable separation, but the means of union gladly willed and accepted. Again and again he compares suffering to red roses, the flowers of love. " For even if there were no other good in suffering than to become more and more like the beautiful clear mirror of Christ, it were well worth while." And so by heavenly alchemy suffering is transformed into joy, and the soul pours forth her delight and thanksgiving to the heavenly Lover : " Behold, how tender, how lovely, how sweet and infinitely good it is to love. Oh, all ye hearts, why do we not love the lovable Lover who cannot but take away sorrow, deliver our hearts, and bring us joy ? Blessed, blessed is the soul that thou, tender Lord, hast chosen to rest in thee."

Rest in the Lord did, at last, come to him, *Unio Mystica*, the goal to which all his service was designed to lead. For Suso was not for nothing the disciple of Master Eckhart, the metaphysician of the Mystic Union. He knew, as all great mystics before and after him, that all his visions, all his loving intercourse with the heavenly beings, were but a " prelude of Divine consolation with which God sometimes entices the beginner." The consummation of the mystic life lies much deeper than in this realm of imaginary visions. It is, in Suso's own words, " a medium-less beholding of the pure Godhead (though not, of course, in the sense of the Beatific Vision) and a vision is the nobler the more intellectual and image-less, and the more like this pure beholding it is." For " the highest end of devout prayer is an immediate union of the soul, when all her faculties are recollected, and when, with pure vision, ardent love, and sweet fruition she is drowned in the pure abyss of the eternal Good, forgetting all things except this pure good." Here Suso has joined the great cloud of witnesses, from Dionysius the Areopagite to St. John of the Cross. Here we are in the realm of the *Ineffabile*, where words fail and images become meaningless. " In the mode-less darkness the manifold vanishes, the spirit loses itself, the reality of self is extinguished."

All his sufferings, all his loving meditations on the Sacred Humanity were but a preparation for this, the Ultimate Reality. Here emotions are stilled, the will is at rest, and the intellect satisfied, for man has at last attained to his true end. God and the soul have found each other in the transforming Union which must for ever defy explanation on this side of the grave.

It is from here, from the sublime heights of this union, that Suso's life derives its full meaning. Without this, his companionship with Saints and Angels might seem the sweet but fanciful play of an artist's imagination, and his rigorous ascetical practices and his love for the red roses of suffering but the outcome of a morbid desire for pain. But before he died, just at the Biblical age, he had reached the peaks of the spiritual life. And we must look to the peaks if we would understand the life of the mystic, for only if seen from there will all the diverse parts fall into place. The *Per Christum Hominem* must be followed by the *Ad Christum Deum*. And conversely we shall never attain to *Christum Deum* unless we have first taken our share in *Christo Homine*. Every other way but The Way leads the mystic astray. For Suso, therefore, the Manhood and the Godhead are the two poles of the mystic life. The Crucifix that begins to speak and the last illumination that leaves man dumb came to him, the Knight-errant and Minnesinger, as they came to his master, the *Confessor et Ecclesiae Doctor Communis.*

CHAPTER III

THREE CHILDREN OF ST. FRANCIS

The Doctor : St. Bonaventure

DEVOTION to the Sacred Humanity, especially to the Divine Child and to the Suffering Christ, has not always played the prominent part in the life of the Church that it plays to-day. Its full development was reserved to the Middle Ages, and perhaps no other Order has had so large a share in it as that of the Saint of Assisi. St. Francis, who in his life imitated the poverty of Bethlehem, and who bore in his body the Stigmata of the Passion, bequeathed both to his Order ; for the Crib and the Stations of the Cross are Franciscan devotions, and Franciscan mysticism is nourished on the spiritual realities whose outward signs they are.

It is the privilege of the Order that its greatest doctor left a series of *opuscula* which deal *ex professo* with the spiritual life, of which the *De Triplici Via, Itinerarium Mentis in Deum, Soliloquium* and *Vitis Mystica* are especially important. It is interesting to recall that nearly all his mystical works were written when he was General of his Order, inundated with an overwhelming multiplicity of absorbing occupations and controversies—one more instance of the apparent paradox that the most outstanding mystics flourish in the storm and stress of " Life " rather than in the uneventful seclusion of the cloister.

In order to understand rightly the doctrine of the Seraphic Doctor two facts must be kept in mind : first, that his approach is theological, not psychological, secondly (we had almost written : consequently) that he regards the ecstatic union as the legitimately desirable goal of the spiritual life. His spiritual doctrine no less than his speculative theology bears the imprint of his " exemplarism." For him the Church on earth is the—imperfect—replica of the Heavenly Jerusalem, to which our mind reaches out in contemplation. Now " in the highest of the celestial hierarchies we distinguish a threefold order, namely Thrones, Cherubim and Seraphim. He, therefore, who would attain to this beatitude

65

must, as far as possible, provide for himself a likeness of these three even in this life (*in via*), so that he may have the quietude of peace, the splendour of truth, and the sweetness of charity. For in these three God Himself has His rest." The spiritual life here on earth, then, is modelled on the angelic choirs of Heaven, and even on the eternal life of the Triune God—a doctrine which prepares us for the lofty heights on which moves the thought of the great Franciscan.

His *De Triplici Via*, in which he traces the ascent of the soul from the Purgative through the Illuminative to the Unitive Way, represents the traditional three stages as a continuity in which the soul must progress from one to the other and not rest until she has reached the state of ecstasy (*excessus*), in which she is at last allowed to say : " It is good for us to be here. And this must be the term of our prayer, nor ought we to desist from it before (we have reached it)."

But before the soul attains to this blessed state she must travel by a long and arduous road. In the Purgative Way she is goaded on by the prick of conscience (*conscientiae stimulus*) which causes her to remember her sins, to acquire knowledge of herself, and to direct her thoughts to what is good. St. Bonaventure's demands are very severe. All natural appetites must be firmly held back ; not only is it reprehensible to consent to the desire for delicious food and fine raiment, but a man should even suppress the first motion of such a desire. Equally to be shunned is the desire for favour, praise or honour, " all of which are vain and make a man vain, and hence are to be avoided as much as the love of women." " But a man should keep his gaze fixed on three things : as regards the future on the day of his death, for the past on the Blood of the Cross, and for the present on the face of the Judge."

These are the realities always present to medieval man : Death, Redemption and Judgment. Without their constant remembrance no spiritual life is possible. But what has become of them in our world ? Though we live, perhaps more than men at any other time, in constant danger of death, we keep our eyes closed, or if we open them, it is only to snatch a little more from the pleasures of this life while there is yet time. For death, to most of us, even to those who are Christians, means an end, not a beginning. There may even be faith in the realities of the future life, but it is hardly more than an intellectual assent, something vaguely believed in, that fails to influence our life here and now. To live *sub specie aeternitatis* is not a characteristic of the twentieth century—but it was the dominating factor of the thirteenth. Only if a soul constantly remembers these great facts of the invisible world, will she be able, as St. Bonaventure demands, to overcome her negligence by strenuous action, her concupiscence by severity, and her malice by benignity. For " benignity, which is a certain sweetness of soul, excludes all malice and disposes the soul to benevolence, forbearance and interior joy." The form of prayer in this way is meditation, in which the soul must " progress from one subject to the other and remain thus until she perceives a tranquillity and serenity from which arises spiritual sweetness ; when this has been reached the mind is quick to tend upwards," that is to say meditation has done its work and the Illuminative Way begins.

As the Purgative Way is dominated by the " prick of conscience," so the next stage in the spiritual life is characterized by the Ray of Intelligence, the *Radius Intelligentiae.* For in the Illuminative Way light is given to the soul on the great mysteries of the Christian Revelation, and she learns " that God has given us His Son for our Brother and Friend, for the price (of our salvation), and that He gives Him daily for our food : the first in the Incarnation, the second in the Passion, the third in the Consecration (of the Host) . . .," further, " that He has given us the Holy Ghost for the sign of our acceptation, the privilege of our adoption, the ring of our espousals. For He has made the Christian soul His friend, His daughter and His spouse." For after the realization of the awful justice of God in the Purgative, comes the blessed assurance of His mercy in the Illuminative Way. Here again, how seldom do Christians realize all the glorious heritage that is theirs. Christ our companion through His Incarnate Life, our justice through His Suffering and Death, our very food in the Holy Eucharist, and to crown it all, the Holy Ghost the pledge of eternal life in the centre of our soul. If you had known the gift of God. . .

The soul, thus purified and illumined, is ready to enter on the Unitive Way, the *Via Perfectiva*, whose emblem is the Spark of Wisdom, the *Igniculum Sapientiae.* Here love is withdrawn from every creature and wholly directed towards God, for here the "two principles, God and the soul, are to be united to each other," from which union springs " true wisdom, in which is knowledge through true experience."

It is the characteristic of Catholic mysticism, in contrast to most of its Protestant counterfeits, that " experience " comes not at the beginning, but at the end of the road. Only after a rigorous moral and mental discipline which curbs the vain curiosity of the mind no less than the appetites of the lower instincts, is the soul ready to enjoy that experimental union with God toward which all her previous training had been directed, and where, inflamed with love, she is raised above all things sensible, imaginable and intelligible to the realm of Divine Wisdom.

Into this outline of the Three Ways St. Bonaventure sketches his magnificent teaching on prayer and the love of God. There are three steps in prayer : grieving for our misery, imploring mercy, and offering adoration, and these ought always to go together. Of them the offering of adoration, *exhibitio latriae,* is the most important ; for through it the attention is withdrawn from ourselves and directed entirely to God, the surest way to achieve holiness, though, in our subjective age, the most difficult to walk in. In this prayer of adoration there is a threefold movement : first our heart bows down in reverence, then it dilates in gratitude, and lastly it is raised up to complacency and mutual colloquy between the Spouse and the bride, " in which, if rightly made, there is a wondrous exultation and jubilation, which leads the soul into ecstasy."

Ecstasy holds the central place in St. Bonaventure's spiritual teaching as the goal towards which our whole life ought to tend ; his various systems of grades and scales, usually arranged in threes, sixes and sevens, all lead up to this. They are almost always set out very briefly and require to be meditated in order to unfold the richness of their meaning. There is, for example, this concise description of the three stages of complacency in God : " In the first the world is crucified to man, in the second man is crucified to the world, in the third man is crucified *for* the world, so that he desires to die for all men, in order that they, too, may be pleasing to God. And this is the state and grade of perfect charity, before the attainment of which no man should consider himself to be perfect."

The entire development of the relations between the soul and the world is summed up in this short passage. For the first stage,

crucifigitur mundus homini, contains all that will later be called the
" active purifications," all that a man can do by his own efforts
to wean himself from the world, all the penances he inflicts on
himself, the sacrifices he makes in order to break the charm of
earthly things. The second stage, in which *homo crucifigitur mundo,*
sums up the " passive purifications," in which God is the principal
agent. Here man is crucified in flesh and spirit, presented to the
world as one completely severed from it, a " spectacle " that the
world no longer comprehends. When the soul has gone through
this crucible she is ready to accomplish the task for which these
first two " crucifixions " have prepared her ; for now *crucifigitur
homo pro mundo.* This is the summit of perfection, because it is
the Christ life. The man who is purified to such a degree has no
more need to make satisfaction for his own faults, but can offer
his penances and sufferings wholly for the sins of others and the
good of the Church.

St. Bonaventure, it is true, is an uncompromising preacher of
the Cross ; but he preaches as eloquently the joy that comes by it.
For at the same time as the soul is enduring her " crucifixions,"
she recovers the Spiritual Senses and ascends the Six Steps of Divine
Love. The believing and loving soul " recovers the spiritual
hearing and sight. The hearing, in order to take in the words of
Christ, the sight in order to consider the splendour of His light.
When she sighs, hoping to receive the in-breathed Word (*Verbum
inspiratum*) . . . she recovers the spiritual sense of smell, and when she
lovingly embraces the Incarnate Word, receiving from Him
delectation and passing into Him by ecstatic love, she recovers taste
and touch." Of these spiritual senses the first two, hearing and
sight, belong to the beginnings of the spiritual life ; they refer not
to such extraordinary phenomena as locutions and visions, but to
the normal activities of Christians, the reading of Scripture and the
listening to instruction combined with meditation, by which the
mind is enlightened. The development of the spiritual " smell "
signifies a deeper penetration, the ardent longing of the soul for a
closer union with the Word ; and the last two stages, taste and
touch, the two senses that immediately unite a man with the object
of his desire, signify possession, that is to say the mystical life in
its fulness.

The Six Steps of Divine Love give the development of the
spiritual life in yet another series of stages. The first of them is

suavitas—what modern authors would call " sensible sweetness,"
which teaches the soul to " taste and see that the Lord is sweet."
The second step is *aviditas*, " for when the soul begins to become
accustomed to this sweetness, there arises in her a great hunger so
that nothing can satisfy her unless she possess perfectly Him Whom
she loves." Once the soul has begun to taste this Divine sweetness
she desires more and more of this spiritual food ; creatures lose
their savour, and the soul experiences a constant desire for the joys
of prayer. If we attempt to fit this state into the modern schemes
of prayer it may perhaps best be classed with the " prayer of
affection," when the soul, filled with sensible devotion, develops
a veritable hunger for prayer and desires to spend hours alone with
her Beloved. In the third stage there comes a break. This is
the state of " satiety (*saturitas*), which proceeds from avidity. For,
as the soul desires God so vehemently and is carried upward,
all that holds her down causes her disgust." Here the soul has
arrived at a turning point of the spiritual life, hovering, as it were,
between heaven and earth, desiring the one and yet held down
by the other. In order to break the thread that holds her back
she must follow the Cross and resolutely ascend the fourth step,
which the Saint calls *ebrietas*, inebriation, where " she should make
torment her consolation and, for the sake of Him Whom she loves,
delight in pain, disgrace and affliction." These are the sufferings
of the " Night of the Spirit " which prepare the soul for the fifth
and sixth stages, which bear the blessed names of " security " and
" tranquillity." In the one, *securitas*, " the soul is so filled with
confidence in the Divine assistance that she believes it impossible
for her to be separated from God." And " the sixth grade is the
true and full tranquillity, in which there is such peace and rest
that the soul is, in some way, in silence and slumber, and, as it were
placed in the ark of Noe, where she can be in no wise disturbed.
For who can disturb a mind that no sting of cupidity disquiets
and no pang of fear agitates ? In such a mind there is peace and
the ultimate state of tranquillity."

For St. Bonaventure ecstasy and peace are almost synonymous.
In his teaching ecstasy *is* peace, and true peace cannot be had without
ecstasy. The deep bliss of the ecstatic soul consists not in the
rigidity of the limbs or the magnificence of visions, but in the
profound tranquillity that invades her and makes her exclaim :
It is good for us to be here. Peace and tranquillity, these are the

goal of the spiritual life. St. Bonaventure, the General of the Franciscans, whose time is occupied with the affairs of his Order from morning to night, can never stress this enough. We, many of us, speak and write of Catholic Action, and when we look at the results of our activities we feel, perhaps, disappointed that so much effort produces so little. St. Bonaventure, like all true mystics, has the disconcerting habit of preaching contemplation instead of action, of spending every free minute of his time in prayer, and of producing, almost unintentionally, results that surpass the wildest dreams of our " activists." Whether we take St. Bernard or St. Teresa, St. Catherine or St. Francis de Sales, there they are, rapt in ecstasy, spending whole nights in prayer, telling the world that union with God is the only thing worth living for, and succeeding, as a kind of by-product, in founding and reforming Orders, directing European politics, and exercising an influence not easily to be gauged on hundreds and thousands of men and women not only of their own, but also of future times.

The explanation of this phenomenon is very simple—so simple, in fact, that it finds little favour with our sophisticated contemporaries. It is nothing else but that the mystics, being entirely surrendered to God, are perfect instruments in His Hands, with which His Wisdom can work as it wills. If we are full of our own plans, desiring things to work out as we want them, " Catholic Action " will accomplish very little, because it is mere human activity for religious purposes. But if we give our whole being to God, asking Him to use us according to His good pleasure, no matter whether, measured by human standards, the end be failure or success—then, indeed, will our work be truly " Catholic Action," because it will be God's action in a human being perfectly surrendered to Him in prayer—and it is only in and through prayer that we can surrender ourselves to Him.

How is this state to be reached where, as St. Bonaventure says, " a man feels himself protected under the shadow of the Divine wings " ? The Saint gives the answer, concise and simple, which may well take one's breath away : *ad quod non potest (homo) per-venire nisi per appetitionem martyrii*—" to which a man cannot attain except through the desire of martyrdom." In other words, for the peace of contemplation heroic sanctity is needed—and the reverse is also true, heroic sanctity cannot be had without contemplation.

Is this elevated view of contemplation meant to deter souls from aiming at it ? Just the contrary ; St. Bonaventure never tires of spurring men on to desire it. On no account should souls be timid where their perfection is at stake, "for God is no accepter of persons. He does not weigh the nobility of race, nor the length of time, nor the number of works, but only the more generous fervour and the greater charity of the devout mind. For He considers not what you once were, but what you have now begun to be." All that is needed to become a contemplative is good will and generosity, for, as St. Bonaventure writes in the *Itinerarium*, "according to the first creation of his nature, man was made apt for the quiet of contemplation" because he was made in the image of God.

We have seen already in the case of St. Bernard that the mystics, though they are the humblest of men where their personal merits are concerned, yet hold the highest view of human nature as created by God. Despite all the modern talk of the rights of men the dignity of the human soul is acknowledged hardly anywhere outside the Church. For it depends on belief in the Triune God and in the statement of *Genesis* that man was made in His image. Once this dogma is given up, what is there in man to command respect ? When we look around us we may, perhaps, be tempted to lose sight of the dignity of the human soul altogether. Greed, lust, ambition—the machinations of financiers, of the divorce courts, of party politicians—what do we see around us to teach us that man bears in his soul the imprint of his Maker—may we not sometimes even be led to doubt that he has an immortal soul at all ? Yet, though we had nothing but dark faith to teach us the dignity of the human soul we ought to be satisfied. But God, in His mercy, has given us proofs that cannot be gainsaid. He has manifested the power and beauty of the God-indwelt soul in His Saints. When we turn our gaze from the easy-going world-without-God of cinema and news-sheets to the transfixed ecstatic of Mount Alvernia whom even the mute creation obeyed, we realize a change of spiritual climate more staggering than the difference between the atmosphere in a coal pit and the clear air on an Alpine peak. Yet both are " air "—only the one is polluted and the other wonderfully pure. So it is with the souls of men : in many sin has obscured the Image almost beyond recognition ;

but in some it is clearly visible, bright and glorious, for they have been perfectly purified even in this life.

How, then, can the Image be restored to its original brightness ? The Franciscan Doctor knows no surer and shorter way than the Way of the Cross. " Consider what He suffers, and behold the ray of Truth through the eye of contemplation ; for by the Passion of the Lamb the seven seals of the Book have been opened." " The desirable Paradise is manifested by the Cross, in which is the summit of all glory . . . when God, in order to restore to us this habitation, was made man for us, vile, miserable and poor." There is no other way to the peace of the Mystic Union than the constant contemplation of the Suffering Christ. For, as we have seen before, the mystic life is the flowering of the gift of Wisdom, and the school of Wisdom is the Cross, to the Jews a scandal and to the Greeks foolishness, but to them that are called the Wisdom of God. For the Cross alone can overcome the great enemy of the soul, *caro tua infelix et misera*, " your unhappy and miserable flesh" as St. Bonaventure calls it.

This is perhaps the greatest obstacle to the spirit of contemplation in our world, the modern attitude to the " Flesh," to the body, so diametrically opposed to that of Christian antiquity and the Middle Ages. For, though the Church has always insisted against the Dualist heresies that the body, being created by God, is in itself something good, yet the teaching of Our Lord Himself and of His Apostles as well as common experience leave no doubt that after the Fall it has become rebellious, refusing to obey the commands of reason, " lusting against the spirit" and defeating it whenever the latter is off its guard. Therefore progress in the spiritual life is impossible unless the body be constantly in some way subdued. But this is precisely what modern man is most unwilling to do. For him the body is not only not an enemy to be conquered, but a dear friend to be pampered and looked after, whose every whim is anxiously attended to. Leaning back in an armchair, cigarette in hand, with a softly crooning wireless beside him, the modern man will tell you that our breathless, noisy life is penitential enough without any extra austerities— our nerves could not stand a fast or a hair shirt. May that, perhaps, be one of the reasons why God permits in our time the horrors of concentration camps, air war and atom bombs ? Is it, perhaps, the reply of Providence to a generation that has become so soft

that the mere mention of a discipline makes them shudder?
Deliciae carnales non possunt esse cum sapientia—" carnal delights
cannot go together with Wisdom " says St. Bonaventure—this
is why there is so little wisdom in our world.

But once a Christian faces squarely the fact that at the centre
of his religion is the Sufferer hanging on the Cross, his attitude
to the body will change. Before the Crucified Body of the
Godman how can he still pamper his own body, his Brother Ass,
as St. Francis calls it? Before the thorn-crowned head and the
pierced hands and feet how can he still make ease and comfort
the main pursuit of his life? No, once a soul has really fallen in
love with Christ she will long to subdue her body, not only to
weaken its resistance to the spirit, but also to make it more closely
resemble Our Lord.

St. Bonaventure's spirituality centres in the Sacred Humanity,
which he calls " the ladder that repairs the first ladder that had
been broken in Adam," by which we can once more enter paradise.
"O Lord Jesus," he prays, "who, for my sake, didst not spare Thyself,
wound my heart with Thy wounds and inebriate my soul with
Thy Blood; that, wherever I turn, I may always see Thee crucified
for me, and that, whatever I behold, may always appear to me
reddened by Thy Blood." And in the contemplation of the
Suffering Saviour in the beautiful *Vitis Mystica* he penetrates, like St.
Gertrude and St. Catherine, into the wound of love that reveals
the Sacred Heart and leads to the closest union between Creator
and creature. " For His Heart is also mine—I say it boldly. For,
if Christ is my head, how then should not what belongs to my
head also belong to me? Therefore, just as the eyes of my bodily
head are truly mine, so also is the heart of my spiritual head mine.
Thus it is well with me : for behold, I have one heart with
Jesus—and why should that seem strange? Since also the multitude
of the faithful were one heart." Here the Sacred Heart is as closely
as possible linked to the doctrine of the Mystical Body : the
Heart of Christ is the heart of the mystic, and the heart of the
mystic is also the heart of the faithful, the heart of Christ's Mystical
Body, which is the Church. For in medieval mysticism the
praying soul is never only the alone with the Alone. She always
feels herself also as the representative of all Christians, praying
perhaps, physically alone, but spiritually in fullest union with
the Church.

It is a great loss that, since the time of the Reformation, there has been a certain rift between public and private prayer, the champions of the one having tended to deprecate the champions of the other. But, as we shall see in the teaching of St. Gertrude, one ought to complement and enrich the other. Precisely because we are all members of the one Body, meant to worship God and sanctify ourselves *within* that Body, must we both receive from and contribute to, the corporate prayer of this Body. We receive from it, because our private prayer will be disciplined, given vigour and " body," so to speak, through the public prayer of the Church, whereas this public prayer, in its turn, will be spiritualized and deepened if the members bring to it the riches of their private contemplation. For the true mystic is never " isolationist." He loves, indeed, silence and solitude, but, being perfected in the growing union with his Creator, his charity cannot but overflow to His creatures, for in them all " you see, hear, praise, love and worship our God," as the disciple of St. Francis expresses it. Isolation is barren, but solitude, the solitude in which the seed of self-love dies, is immensely fruitful. " Let us therefore die," says St. Bonaventure, "and enter into the darkness ; let us impose silence on solicitude, concupiscence and phantasms, and let us pass with Christ crucified from this world to the Father. . . ."

The Penitent : Bl. Angela de Foligno

THE Order of St. Francis glories in two remarkable women Saints who were penitents : St. Margaret of Cortona and Bl. Angela de Foligno ; perhaps even in three, if St. Catherine of Genoa, as there is good reason to believe, was also a Franciscan Tertiary. If we marvel at the miracles of grace God works in such seraphic virgins as St. Catherine of Siena or St. Teresa, these seem even more striking against a background of sin, as it appears in the lives of those great mystics whom Divine grace took by the hair, so to speak, in a few days or even in a moment, changing their sinful passion into the burning fire of Divine Love.

Bl. Angela of Foligno, who was born about 1249, had lived a very worldly and culpable life till she was about forty years old.

Then she was suddenly converted—in what way we do not know—
became a Tertiary of St. Francis, and was apparently almost from
the beginning favoured with high graces. From that time onwards her mystical life is richly documented owing to the care of
her confessor, who wrote down in Latin what she dictated to him
in the vernacular. Though she complained that what he had
written seemed very dry and lifeless to her as compared with the
reality she was trying to convey, we have both his and her own
word for it that he added nothing of his own, and the elevation
and surety of doctrine of this remarkable penitent were admired
by such authorities as St. Francis de Sales and St. Alphonsus de
Liguori. Her life seems truly an illustration of St. Bonaventure's
saying that God takes not into account what a man has once been.
His grace can raise even the greatest sinner to the heights of the
mystical life, provided he responds to the Divine call with sufficient
generosity.

There is, however, a mark which ordinarily distinguishes the
mystic who is a penitent from the one who has never lost his
Baptismal innocence. It is a certain violence with which he turns
against his natural instincts, an unmeasured hatred of the old self
which will often—as in Angela's case—lead to embarrassing scenes
and retard the progress of calm and serenity that usually
accompanies the development of the mystical life. On the other
hand, the mystics who are penitents will teach us the meaning of
real penitence with more force and conviction than any other men,
because only in mystical contemplation is the soul given the full
knowledge of the heinousness of sin, which she sees in the light of
Divine Love manifested in the Cross.

In a penetrating analysis Bl. Angela traces the " Twenty Steps
of Penitence " by which she herself was led into the way of sanctity.
After the first imperfect knowledge and confession of sin, she makes
full satisfaction, realizes the Divine mercy, and begins to be
" illumined." This illumination plunges her into deep grief,
her desire for penance is increased, and she enters on the dolorous
way of self-knowledge, seeing " nothing in herself save faults."
Then she receives a " certain illumination of grace, in which I was
given a profound knowledge of all sins. And in this illumination
I saw that I had offended all creatures that were made for me, and
my sins were poignantly recalled to my memory. . . And then
it was granted to me to pray with great ardour of love."

These are the two main factors of all true penitence : knowledge of self and love of God ; without the one penitence would be an empty formality, without the other it would turn into despair. Out of the bitter root of penance and shame springs the sweet flower of love, which soon finds abundant nourishment in the Cross. And the first fruit of this flower, which makes her feel that she herself has crucified her Lord, is the vow of chastity, from which her nature shrinks, "for on the one hand I was afraid to promise, and on the other the fire of love compelled me to promise, and I could not do otherwise."

I could not do otherwise. . . Does this mean that she was no longer free to refuse the invitation of grace ? It is a common element in all great conversions that there comes a moment when the soul feels herself constrained to follow the attraction of grace which seems irresistible, though she is at the same time conscious of her freedom to reject it. When theologians speak of " prevenient grace " and " physical premotion," these terms may sound abstruse—but to an Angela de Foligno they would only be the theological interpretation of a lived experience, and it is not without significance that these conceptions are precisely the elaboration of the teaching of the greatest converts of the Church, St. Paul and St. Augustine.

After the gift of her chastity the work of grace becomes even more evident. " And I was to seek the way of the Cross and to give my heart to Christ, and to go by a thorny road, that is, by tribulation." But she could not follow this call while she was living with her husband, her mother and children, who had claims on her. Therefore she did what will probably always cause scandal to many : she began to pray for their death. And her prayer was heard : one after the other they all died. " And, because I had started on the way I spoke of before and had asked God that they should die, I received great consolation from their death."

Shall we turn in horror from this recital, sounding the more revolting to us because it is made in such a bare, matter-of-fact way, as if it were quite an ordinary thing for a mother to pray for the death of her family and to derive consolation from it ? We have to admit that to pray for the death of a person who seems to be an obstacle to our spiritual life is wrong under all circumstances except in response to an irresistible Divine inspiration—but it may safely be said that this exception is so rare as to be almost unique. The ordinary way with which we meet over and over again in the lives of the Saints is that either the obstacles are removed by Divine Providence without the co-operation or even the desire of the person concerned—so e.g. in the cases of St. Margaret of Cortona and of St. Jeanne Françoise de Chantal, or that the apparent obstacle becomes itself a powerful means of sanctification, as in the case of Bl. Anna Maria Taigi. Yet God is free to accomplish His designs in the way He pleases, and that Angela's prayer was made in response to a Divine inspiration is sufficiently proved by the extraordinary series of deaths that followed it. Nor was it made in harmony with her natural desires. When, a little later, she describes some intense suffering she writes : "And to live was even more painful to me than the death of mother and sons (*Et vivere erat mihi pœna super dolorem mortis matris et filiorum*)." Her prayer, then, was made in obedience to the Will of God and against her natural feelings, and the "consolation" she experienced when those she loved were taken from her was entirely supernatural : the sweetness often accorded to a soul that has sacrificed all earthly love for her Heavenly Spouse.

The ways of the God who spared not His only-begotten Son must necessarily often remain dark to our limited human reason though we may come nearer to understanding them in this partcular case if we reflect that for a woman who had lived in sin till her fortieth year to reach the mystical heights the school of detachment and suffering must needs be far harder than for others. The exceptional demands made on her by God soon showed themselves in the practice of superhuman penance and in the complete renunciation of all worldly possessions, deemed imprudent even by her Franciscan directors, who considered her still too young to go begging. There follows an excellent account of the gradual illumination of the soul. She begins to understand the Pater Noster, the eternal prayer that has inspired some of the most beautiful pages of St. Thomas and St. Teresa, in an entirely new way : "He put into my heart the Pater Noster, with a clear understanding of the Divine goodness, and my own unworthiness ; and the individual words were explained to me in my heart . . . and I began to taste something of the Divine goodness," a typical description of contemplative prayer, which is infused, not reached by the activity of human thought, and accompanied by a " taste," a spiritual enjoyment which has an irresistible attraction for the soul favoured with it. Her faith, too, is in some way changed, "so that the faith I had hitherto had seemed as it were dead in comparison." She is given a new understanding of the Gospels, which fills her with light and love, " and I began to have constantly, whether waking or sleeping, a Divine sweetness in my soul."

Thus she has arrived at the threshold of the mystical life, in which illumination of the intellect is combined with the powerful attraction of the will to God, expressing itself in a felt "sweetness," which quickly detaches the soul from all earthly desires. Her prayer becomes more and more intense, until she loses the power of speech, a frequent phenomenon of contemplative prayer and part of the so-called "ligature." It usually begins to make its appearance with the "Prayer of Quiet" and prevents voluntary movements, when it is very strong even the exercise of sight and hearing. At last Angela's directors, convinced of the reality of the Divine operations in her soul, agree that she may divest herself of all her property. With this act of perfect imitation of her holy Father St. Francis she has reached the twentieth step of penitence and is ready to enter on the life of union.

This new life is described in a sequence of seven steps. The arrangement in steps and "ladders" has been a favourite device of the mystics from early times, when St. Benedict in the West and St. John Climacus in the East wrote the Twelve Steps of Humility (in the Benedictine Rule) and the Scala Paradisi. Angela begins with the revelatio divinæ familiaritatis, the revelation of the Holy Trinity and of Our Lord in the Blessed Sacrament, the fundamental doctrines of the inner life of the Godhead and the extension of the Incarnation in the consecrated Host. It cannot be repeated too often that Catholic mysticism is really only lived dogma. The mystics are saturated with the doctrines of the Church, which, far from being a kind of Procrustean bed as most Protestants assume, are the very air they breathe, without which their spiritual life would wither away and become that vague emotional pantheism that nowadays so often usurps the name of Mysticism. As if to leave no doubt on her meaning Angela describes " the revelation of the Divine education through doctrines (documenta) perceived by the ear, and through doctrines intelligible only to the taste of the mind (gustu mentis)." Some of these doctrines are further specified—they are precisely those most unpalatable to human pride, viz., "the revelation of human humiliation and of the Divine reformation and acceptance. And in this step is contained how she saw the whole world and all things as something very small and God filling and exceeding all," a vision reminding us of Mother Julian. At last she sees in a rapture (*in raptu mentis*) "the power of God and the Will of God, by which she was satisfied on every question, namely on all those who will be saved and who are saved, and on the damned and the demons . . . and she remained contented . . . but she knew not whether she was then in the body or out of the body."

Here again we meet the intellectual element which plays so important a part in all authentic mysticism. Those ultimate mysteries of salvation and damnation are made comprehensible in some manner by an illumination that produces rapture. There is, then, in ecstasy, an intense intellectual activity, though in a purely receptive way, that is to say the intellect is filled with a new kind of knowledge on the mysteries of the Faith, a knowledge which it will retain in its normal state and which, though inexpressible in human words, will show itself in an increase of the gifts of Wisdom and Understanding.

It is very necessary to insist on this intellectual aspect of the mystical life, because its frequent external concomitants so closely resemble a swoon or even a profound coma, and because, moreover, the language of the mystics themselves who speak about Divine darkness, ignorance, unknowing, etc., would seem to suggest that ecstasy is a state of unconsciousness and mental "blackout," as it were. But all the mystics, from Pseudo-Dionysius, or rather from St. Paul, onwards, are at one in telling us that what they call "darkness" is really an excess of light, which appears dark to them only because the human intellect is so weak. Nor is it surprising that the physical effects should be so misleading. For even a very intense intellectual absorption in the natural sphere often produces a partial insensibility ; the philosopher or the mathematician intent on working out a problem, will neither see nor hear what is happening around him, nor will he realize that the time for dinner is long past. How much more intense will these phenomena be in the mystic, whose intellect is being absorbed by the Supreme Intellect Himself, under whose impact all the normal activities of the body cease while the soul is wholly occupied with receiving the infusion of supernatural light.

After Angela has been enlightened on the intellectually difficult mysteries of the Faith there follows " the revelation of the Divine union and love," in which she receives light on the deep mysteries of the love of God for man : on the Passion, which causes her an " excess of love," on the intercession of Our Lady for all mankind, and on the Blessed Sacrament. After this flood of light and consolation comes a martyrdom of body and soul closely corresponding to the descriptions of St. John of the Cross and St. Teresa of the Dark Night of the Spirit and the pains suffered before the Transforming Union.

Bl. Angela, the penitent, is being led to the same heights as the virginal Catherine or Teresa. But because she has been raised so high from the very depths she is constantly afraid of vainglory and pride. The Lord, however, takes good care lest the chosen soul He has delivered from the lust of the flesh should fall into the worse snare of spiritual pride. When the Holy Ghost has just said to her " Love Me, for you are much beloved by Me," and she receives ineffable consolation from these Divine words, " then my sins and vices were at once recalled to my memory, and I felt a greater humility than I had ever done before." For the more closely God unites her to Himself, the more clearly is she made to see her faults, and the more is she afraid lest her mystical experiences should be delusions. This fear, which springs from true humility and knowledge of self, and is one of the surest signs of authentic mysticism, is in Angela's case especially strong because of the sins of her past life and the extraordinary graces she receives. For she is allowed to feel " the Cross corporeally, and by feeling it, my soul was liquefied in the love of God." Soon afterwards the consolations Our Lord showers on her become so ineffable that she lies motionless for eight days, so that " during these days I could hardly speak, nor say a Pater Noster, nor could I rise."

Perhaps such a prolonged state of prostration might seem pathological. But even if this were so—and without in any way disparaging these extraordinary states, we may frankly admit that it looks as if there was a pathological streak in Angela de Foligno— this would in no way detract from the authenticity of her mystical experiences, as little as pathological phenomena in a poet or other creative artist detract from the value of his art. A very highly strung emotional and spiritual life may from time to time show the effects of strain, especially in the state of ecstasy, when the body is not yet adapted to the impact of extraordinary graces ; but these are weaknesses which disappear almost entirely if and when the last stage, the Transforming Union, is reached. For these " pathological" states are only surface phenomena ; if they went deeper, they would affect reason and will. But this is just the fundamental difference between mystics and hysterical persons, that the reason of the former is progressively enlightened, so that even the great ones of this world often seek their advice, and that their will becomes marvellously strong, overcoming all obstacles, whereas the development of the latter is just in the opposite direction.

Shortly after her eight days' rapture Angela received a further increase of graces, which she describes in the second of the Seven Steps. When she wanted to say the Pater Noster " a voice came into my soul saying : You are full of God. And then I felt all the members of my body full of the delight of God . . . and I felt how God embraced my soul." Yet, however great her joy in this Divine familiarity, her sins came always to her mind, " and I doubted that such great things should actually be said to me." So in her distress she asks God for a sign, a precious stone for example—a favour of which she had no doubt read in the lives of some of the mystics, to convince her that it was truly He Who spoke to her. But He tells her that even such a ring would not rid her of her doubts, because she might be deceived in it. But He proposes to give her a better proof : " And this sign shall be always with you. . . You shall be burning with the love of God . . . and this love will be so fervent that, if someone says something evil to you, you will hold it to be a favour and will exclaim that you are unworthy of such a grace. And this is the certain sign of the grace of God : for thus have I borne (ignominy) with great humility and patience."

It is a very popular misconception that mystics are credulous people always ready to take the figments of their imagination for sober fact. In reality the exact opposite is true. There are no more sceptical persons than the mystics, at least where their own mystical favours are concerned. They know, indeed, that they have had some extraordinary experiences, but they are only too eager to seek advice, being fully alive to the danger of illusion and diabolic interference. But habitually to bear insults with humility and to face sufferings with joy is impossible to human nature except by the powerful assistance of grace, and such a reproduction of the Christ-life in a soul is the best proof of the reality of her mystical life, for by their fruits you shall know them.

The sign that God has promised Angela appears in her increased desire for suffering ; she now lives to the full the life of contemplation, to which St. Bonaventure ascribes the longing for martyrdom. She receives an intellectual vision of a very high order, for she sees God as " a plenitude, a clarity, through which I felt in myself an indescribable fulness. . . I can say nothing else but that it was altogether beauty and goodness." This, of course, does not mean that she has seen the Divine Essence, but some of His attributes, beauty and goodness, conveyed in an ineffable impression of plenitude and light. The term " vision," though generally used in Mystical Theology even for such principally intellectual experiences, is somewhat misleading, because it gives the general reader the idea of something " seen " by the eye of the imagination. But such graces are really far more subtle ; they are intellectual illuminations in which the imagination plays only a very subordinate part, just sufficient to enable the soul who is still in her earthly body to grasp the truth that is being impressed on the intellect.

The constant interplay of intellectual illumination and the ardour of love, one being increased by the other, is very striking in Angela's writings. So in the next, the Third Step, she rises to even greater heights of charity : " My heart was lifted up above all earthly things and placed in God, so that I could neither think nor see anything save God. And whether I talked or eat or whatever I did, nothing could prevent my heart from being always in God." This state of happiness is followed by four weeks of black desolation, when " I stood in tribulation, and I seemed to feel nothing of God, and it seemed to me that I was so to speak forsaken by God." But after the brief Night is over consolations increase. She feels herself embraced by Christ and enters into His Side— and after these proofs of His Love she receives again lights of a very high order : she " sees " the ineffable power and will of God, " in which I understood most fully and with certainty all the things about which I had asked," a knowledge which fills her with such delight that it overflows into the body.

In the " Fifth Step " she is granted the " revelation of the Divine Union and Love." Though she describes experiences similar to preceding ones, such as more visions of the Divine essence (as far as it can be "seen" in this life) and profound ecstasies, it is clear from her accounts that they are of a more exalted nature, and their reality is confirmed by their effects; for her confessor is constrained to express his amazement at her perfect confessions and contrition. She describes very clearly the effects by which she recognizes the Divine Presence in her soul, speaking of "a certain unction which suddenly renews the soul and softens the limbs of the body (a mystical experience similar to "liquefaction," in which the love felt by the soul overflows into the body making it soft, as it were, and responsive to the Divine action) conforming them to the state of the soul, so that nothing can touch or hurt her." In this state she has not even tears of joy—it is too exalted for that, for "God brings with Him into the soul such a superabundance of gladness that she has nothing more to ask for." Her confessor gives an interesting description of her appearance when in this state : "She became white and red, radiant and joyful, and her eyes so bright that she seemed no longer herself"—a picture the more striking if we remember that she must have been about fifty years old at the time, and weakened by her penances, but which tallies perfectly with descriptions of other mystics, e.g. St. Teresa, in a similar state of exultation.

But, exalted as this state is, she has not yet attained to the stability of the Transforming Union ; for this she has first to pass through a longer and more painful period of complete darkness than those she had to endure before. Her account of it has an extraordinary freshness and vigour : "The torments that the soul has to bear from the devils I can liken to nothing else but to a man hung by the neck, who, blindfolded and with hands bound behind his back, remains alive, suspended by a rope and in irons, with no expectation of support or help." And, changing from this corporeal image to the spiritual condition of the soul in this state, she continues : "All the virtues of the soul are overturned while she herself looks on and knows it." Even worse, "all her vices live again ; not that they are permanently there, still they cause much pain ; and even those vices which were never there enter the body. . . the soul sees that all strength is taken away from her, and though she does not consent, yet she has no power at all to resist these vices."

This is the most searching of the trials of the Dark Night of the

Spirit, that the soul should appear utterly powerless to resist the storm of evil suggestions and desires raging within her.   Actually she does resist all the time by the very fact that she does not consent, and the more strenuous her resistance, the more painful the trial. The onslaught of the powers of evil seems to come from her own unfathomed depths, and this most painful purification teaches her the nothingness of the creature : Without Me you can do nothing.

In this Dark Night " God is completely shut out and hidden from me, so that I cannot even remember Him. . . Hence, seeing my sins, I fight against these devils with all my strength."   But, being unable to prevail against them, " I become full of wrath and sadness, bitter and furious," a state which is the more humiliating as the soul afflicted with these temptations has but the one desire to please God—only to find herself in a condition where she appears to herself most displeasing to Him.   It is only after the turmoil has ceased that she is able to recognize that this " is the greatest purgation and purification of the soul."

When it is at last over, Angela the penitent finds herself on the threshold of the Transforming Union described in the Seventh Step.   It begins with another vision of God, higher than all the former ones, when she sees Him in a darkness, which is darkness only " because He is a greater good than can be thought or understood . . . . and she sees nothing, and she sees all. . . ." As Master Eckhart and so many other mystics she can express the inexpressible only in contradictions.   " And the soul receives a knowledge of God so great that I cannot understand how it comes about," still less can she express it.   At the same time she is introduced to the deepest region of the soul, " where there is neither joy nor sadness nor delectation . . . . but where there is all good and all truth . . . ."

Only very few men and women are privileged in this life to attain to the knowledge of their own souls—for this knowledge depends on the knowledge of God.   As the soul is made in the image of God, so true knowledge of self is proportionate to knowledge of God, for in the mysterious ground of the soul is mirrored the Image of God, " And I see Him Who is Being, and how He is the being of all creatures."   At last she sees herself no longer in herself, but in God ; there is an indescribable note of triumph in the words of the sinner whom God has transformed into a Saint : " And I see myself with God wholly pure, wholly sanctified,

wholly true, wholly upright . . . . and wholly heavenly in Him"
and she hears the words : " In thee rests all the Trinity, all Truth,
so that you hold Me and I hold you." "And," she confesses," to
this state I have been wholly led and elevated by God, for I myself
could neither will, nor desire, nor ask for this state " . . . . " And
my soul could not comprehend herself."

It is a wonderful thing that a woman, who until her fortieth
year had been leading a life of sin, should have been raised to these
heights ; but the words of Truth that there is more joy in heaven
over one sinner who repents than over the ninety-nine just have
at all times been as valid as on the day when Mary Magdalene
washed the Feet of her Lord with her tears. But the way from
sin to the heights of the spiritual life, how can it be found ? Bl.
Angela gives the answer of all the mystics : " I believe that a soul
cannot find this Divine light more quickly nor more easily than by
devout and pure and humble and continuous and ardent prayer."
Prayer, this invisible activity of the soul and in the soul, prayer,
this mysterious relation between God and man that can be as full
of bliss as it can be full of pain, prayer, then, is the way that leads
into the Kingdom of Heaven, and that leads there infallibly,
whether we start from our Baptismal innocence or from a life
that has been immersed in sin. But it is a hard way, for, as the
life of Blessed Angela shows so clearly, once a soul has started on
it she is compelled to divest herself of one attachment after the
other. For the God of the mystic is the same as the God of
Abraham, Isaac and Jacob, He is a jealous God. But He takes
away all only in order to give All, changing the emptiness of sin
into the fulness of grace that is a beginning of eternal life even
in this sinful world.

The Stigmatic : Louise Lateau

WITH Louise Lateau we enter a sphere that differs considerably
from that of the mystics hitherto studied. For she belongs to
that rather small class of contemplatives whose spiritual life is
dominated in a special way by one particular grace, and that a
gratia gratis data. It is perhaps not surprising that the fact of
bearing the Wounds of Christ in one's body should absorb almost

all the spiritual activities of a person, though in some cases, like those of St. Francis and St. Catherine, it is only one mystical favour though an exceptionally great one, beside many others not connected with it. For Louise Lateau, however, as for Maria Moerl, Teresa Neumann and others, it was the one great centre of her mystical life from which all other graces sprang and with which all other extraordinary phenomena were intimately connected.

Louise Lateau was born in 1850 ; her father died soon after her birth and left her mother and two sisters in great poverty. She received next to no education apart from learning to read and write. From the age of eleven, when she made her First Communion, she had to work ; but she always found time for prayer, and seems to have been introduced to a very simple form of contemplation when she was about thirteen. The first striking signs of her sanctity appeared during a cholera epidemic in 1866, when she nursed the sick with great devotion and complete forgetfulness of her own danger. In the same year she was received into the Franciscan Third Order. Her spiritual life now developed rapidly ; after a period of great aridity and anxiety, she seems to have received the Prayer of Quiet together with a special devotion to the Blessed Sacrament and the intense desire to receive It frequently. In 1867, the year of her profession in the Third Order, the " lights " in prayer became more frequent, bearing especially on the Presence of God, the Passion, and the Blessed Sacrament, which remained her principal attractions throughout her life. These " lights " were soon followed by the unmistakable authentication of suffering. She began to be subject to headaches, acute neuralgic pains in her left arm, side and legs, and to abscesses—sufferings which seem to have been the prelude to the Stigmata, which began to appear in 1868. On 3rd January, of that year, exactly eight days before the death of the other Franciscan stigmatic, Maria Moerl, she felt a ray penetrating her soul, causing at first a feeling of great joy, but soon afterwards intense pains that seemed to radiate from her heart into her hands, feet and side. These pains recurred every Friday with increasing intensity until in April of that year blood began to ooze from her side, the next Friday also from her feet, and the week after from the surface of her hands, flowing more abundantly every time. The hæmorrhage usually began on the night from Thursday to Friday and stopped on Friday about five o'clock in the evening. As in the case of other stigmatics who have been under medical observation it was found not to flow from the veins but out of blisters on the epidermis. Despite her sufferings at the time when the wounds were actually bleeding she was in good health during the rest of the week, and could continue her ordinary occupations.

But this does not mean that she herself remained unchanged. After the appearance of the Stigmata her union with God became more profound, and she was habitually recollected. There was another curious phenomen, noticed by those who knew her well : it was the remarkable change in her language, which became ennobled, as it were, and almost inspired. It is a trait common to almost all mystics from all strata of society that the further they advance in the mystical life the purer and more expressive becomes their style. Whether we take the great Spanish, Italian, English or German mystics, the writings of all of them are considered classics and are read, merely for their literary qualities, by many who do not share their faith. Perhaps this is not so difficult to account for if we consider that the mystics are in particularly intimate relationship with the Word. Now the Word is the perfect image and expression of the Father, therefore it is only to be expected that He will bestow on His devoted lovers the capacity for expression, so that their language becomes in a manner worthy of the experiences and teaching they are called upon to convey.

Thus the Lord gave to the poor girl whose body He was more and more conforming to His own a dignity and beauty of bearing and language that surprised those who had known her from child-hood. Very soon her absorption in prayer developed into ecstasy so that she could be roused neither by shaking nor shouting. There was only one means by which to bring her back to her normal state, the so-called " rappel " or " recall." This is one of the most remarkable phenomena of authentic mysticism, and one which completely demolishes the Protestant theory that the mystics are very individualistic people who find the greatest difficulty in bringing their private mystical life into line with the obedience required from them by the Church.

The Recall consists in this, that at a command—whether ex-pressed in words or given only mentally—from the ecclesiastical superior the mystic at once comes out of his ecstasy, which has resisted all natural means, even to the infliction of acute physical pain. This power of Recall, of which there are instances in the lives of many mystics, was used in the case of Louise Lateau in a truly scientific—and incidentally often very cruel—manner. It was employed for example by the doctors investigating the phenomena, with whom it worked whenever the curé or another priest to whom she owed obedience had delegated his authority to them, though not otherwise. There is nothing resembling hypnosis here—the curé was a very ordinary and unimaginative man, and the doctors, in any case, would have been particularly bad subjects for his experiments. It is simply a fact that so far has defied natural explanation that Louise came out of her ecstasy every time when ordered to do so by authority—though often at the cost of great suffering, and returned to it the moment the command was withdrawn.

But, if we accept the supernatural explanation—would it not mean that Almighty God obeys His creatures? It does indeed mean that. And it is really far less wonderful than the " Divine Obedience " on which every priest depends every morning that he says Mass. For it has so pleased Almighty God to give to His Church the power of binding and loosing ; and surely it is no more difficult to recall a person from ecstasy than to give her absolution—only the one can be perceived by the senses and the other can not. But in all these cases, the offering of Mass, sacramental confession, and the " recall," the source of power is the priestly office, which, in its turn, derives from the Priesthood of Christ. Therefore, when the priest exercises his priestly power, he acts as it were officially, by the authority of Christ delegated to him, whereas the mystic, though held in ecstasy by the same Divine power, is thus held only as a private individual, to be released whenever the official representative of this power demands it. For if, as the inspired prophet says, " obedience is better than sacrifice," then *a fortiori* obedience must be better than ecstasy, and in order that he may exercise this high virtue of obedience to lawful authority, Divine Omnipotence releases the mystic from his ecstatic union ; for there is no rapture however exalted that would place him outside the obedience of the Church.

So Louise, impervious to all natural efforts to stop her ecstasies, would at once regain her normal consciousness at the command of Père Huchant, one of the members of the Commission appointed by Cardinal Deschamps in September, 1868, to investigate the phenomena that were beginning to cause a stir throughout Belgium.

Superiors or directors incapable of understanding, or even hostile, are one of the most common sources of affliction to the mystics ; and Louise had her full share of them. The constant recalls from ecstasy which Père Huchant inflicted on her caused her intense suffering. Even in the lower stages of prayer, if it is at all " sweet " and satisfying, the sudden termination of it by some exterior cause is, at least, displeasing. " I adjure you, daughters of Jerusalem . . . . that you rouse not, nor awake my love until it please her." The soul held in the embrace of her God is filled with the most intense happiness possible here on earth, and normally this " embrace " ceases gradually, the union becoming steadily weaker, until it terminates almost imperceptibly. In the case of the " recall " it is different. Without any preparation the soul is suddenly " dropped," as it were, sustaining a spiritual " fall " which hurts as much or more than a physical fall. If this experiment is repeated over and over again, the soul suffers like a man who is perpetually woken up the moment he has gone to sleep.

Nor was this the only trial that Père Huchant devised for her. He frequently gave her orders that contradicted those given by other members of the Commission, and if she failed to carry them out he accused her of disobedience. He made her work on Fridays, hoping that this would prevent the blood flowing from the stigmata, but without success. He also caused her to take food on these days, which she was forced to eject under great pains. When he was at last removed from the Commission Père van Loo, a Recollect, took his place. He, too, was determined to try her spirit to the utmost ; he treated her as if she had made a pact with the devil, and actually told her that she was lost.

But the Lord was more merciful than His ministers. After a particularly trying day He appeared to her, and for the first time spoke to her. " My daughter, why are you discouraged ? " The Divine words effected what they expressed and her spirits were restored.

She needed this reassurance, for she had to suffer not only the attacks of men but also those of the devil. A living faith in God and belief in the devil usually go together ; therefore, since the rationalism of the eighteenth century, the devil has rather gone " out of fashion," and we may be sure that this enlightened opinion, however much it may have hurt his vanity, was of great advantage to him ; for a soul that half-heartedly believes in a God devoid of all mystery and laughs at a fallen archangel is easy prey for Lucifer. It seems as if the very fact of this general unbelief induced him to manifest himself most palpably where it was worth his while. The Curé d'Ars and St. Gemma Galgani are famous for their battles with the devil. The prince of this world does not bother much about mediocrity. But where he suspects sanctity he is on the spot. A young woman who bore in her body the marks of the Wounds that had defeated his power was well worth his while. So he threw Louise about and appeared to her, frequently under revolting animal forms, especially at prayer time. The lives of all the Saints make it clear that he must derive a singular satisfaction from disturbing souls at prayer ; but unknowingly he only furthers God's work in them with these attacks, for the sufferings that his pranks and suggestions cause them only draw them more closely to their Lord.

When Louise emerged from these trials her life became more and more extraordinary. After her stigmatization had been completed, she became gradually unable to take any food at all, not even water. Nevertheless she remained in excellent health and could even do heavy housework. The doctors examined her and certified that her stomach was completely empty of anything, whether solid matter, liquid or gas, and declared themselves unable to give a scientific explanation of the fact. She also ceased to feel heat or cold, and after the appearance of the Crown of Thorns, sleep, too, became impossible, so that in 1873 the bed was removed from her room. How did she pass the weary hours of the night ? " Thank God," she said, " the night passes like the day, so that I hardly perceive anything. It is like a thought which is always the same, and prevents me from telling the time." For from this time she had the habitual vision of the Blessed Trinity, and her soul was already enjoying the foretaste of eternity while her body was still carrying on its works and sufferings in time.

With this superhuman mode of life she also received a form of knowledge that did no longer depend on the evidence of the senses. When in ecstasy she could distinguish objects that were blessed without ever being deceived. If a blessed Rosary, for example, was presented to her, she would grasp it and smile, but if it was not blessed she would remain quite unmoved. This faculty showed itself particularly in the presence of the Blessed Sacrament. Once a box was brought to her containing the Holy

Oils, to which was attached a small pyx, believed to be empty, The moment the box was presented to her Louise knelt down and when it was moved about she followed it on her knees, while her features and movements expressed the greatest delight. The presence of the Holy Oils seemed insufficient to explain this devotion ; so the pyx was detached from the box, which was shown to her alone and did not produce more than a smile ; but when the pyx was once more brought to her she trembled with joy. At last the priest opened it, and to his amazement found that it contained a few particles of the Host.

This knowledge of holy things, technically called hierognosis, goes frequently with stigmatization, and in a case like the one just recounted even the explanation of a possible unconscious suggestion is ruled out, seeing that the presence of the Blessed Sacrament was not suspected by anyone in the room. It seems as if the Lord delights from time to time in confounding the wisdom of the wise by presenting it with a case before which it has either to confess itself defeated, or to declare, in the ultimate despair of pride, like Zola at Lourdes that it will not believe. Louise, too, found her Zola in the person of the famous German physician Virchow, who brought her case before a congress of doctors at Breslau, only to deny the reality of the facts and to declare that the whole thing was a fraud. But, unlike Zola, he refused even to visit the place in which this fraud was being perpetrated, and when, in 1874, the Belgian Academy of Medicine, after a lengthy investigation in which every conceivable precaution was used, declared themselves unable to produce a natural explanation of the phenomena, Virchow and his fellow—rationalists declared the Belgian doctors superstitious fools. An unbelieving age asks for proofs of Divine intervention, and when they are given, receives them as little as Corozain and Bethsaida received the miracles of Our Lord.

Perhaps the greatest marvel of her life apart from the Stigmata themselves was her relationship to the Blessed Sacrament. Already on the day of her First Communion Louise had been unable to take any food, much to the annoyance of her mother, who had prepared a festive meal. As she grew in union with Our Lord, His Body became the one sustenance of her life, on which she relied for the renewal of both her spiritual and her physical strength. This is how she describes Its effects on herself : " When one returns

from the absorption produced by the light (i.e. ecstasy) one has
above all a feeling of love. After Holy Communion, in addition
to the love, one feels a force in the soul, a force so great that it
communicates itself to the body, so that one is no longer conscious
of it, and all bodily suffering vanishes. . . . After Communion
the strength the body has received diminishes gradually, and in
proportion to the time elapsed since Communion. . . . Communion makes one feel changed into Jesus Christ, and affection is
felt especially towards the humanity of Our Lord ; one feels more
tranquil and full of life." On days when she did not communicate
she was very weak and unable to work, but as soon as she had
received the Blessed Sacrament her strength returned, diminishing
once more towards evening. The way in which she communicated was in itself extraordinary : for she did not swallow the
Host but seemed to inhale it, as it were, without the slightest
movements of her throat muscles. After Communion she was
usually in ecstasy for about half an hour : " I feel that Our Lord is
present within me, because I experienced no further desire," and
during this time even the recall caused her no suffering, for it could
not separate her from her Lord, whom she continued to feel
sensibly within her. *Caro enim mea vere est cibus.* . . . If souls
only realised this glorious truth with a living faith, how much more
fruitful would be their Communions. Only few, it is true, are
called to ecstatic union—but who could doubt that the Blessed
Sacrament which contains in Itself all delight would work far
greater marvels in the souls of men if It were received with a deeper
faith and love ? Its full power is revealed in the lives of the mystics,
and their example should spur on others to greater devotion, so
that their souls would be filled with Christ and their lives would
show Him forth.

In an existence so full of extraordinary graces as Louise's the
sufferings, too, will be of an extraordinary character, of peculiar
intensity and produced by invisible agencies, defying the skill of
doctors and psychologists. Like St. Catherine and Bl. Anna
Maria Taigi she was destined to be a victim of expiation for the
good of the Church. She said herself : " I always ask to suffer
for others ; I offer all my sufferings for the Sovereign Pontiff,"
and on his accession Leo XIII asked that she should pray for him
as she had done for Pius IX. In 1870, during the invasion of the
Papal States by the Piedmontese, her sufferings increased, reaching

their climax on the 20th of September, when the enemy troops entered Rome, and continuing till the Feast of the Immaculate Conception. They returned in Holy Week, 1871, during the horrible profanations perpetrated in Paris and Rome ; on Good Friday she was seized with inexplicable exterior and interior pains ; her tongue was swollen, and she seemed in a death agony. In 1873 Our Lord told her to prepare herself for more sufferings, helping her to bear them by many extraordinary favours and an ever closer union with Himself. He showed her the sufferings of His Heart and enlarged her own heart—a phenomenon frequently met with in the lives of the mystics expressing in a sensible manner the increase of charity in a soul.

From 1876 her sufferings grew in intensity. She could no longer go to church, but Communion had to be brought to her house, and from 1879 she was completely bedridden. Her pains were all localised in the regions of the Stigmata, and the more acute they became the greater seemed to grow her strength. She bore them without complaint, offering herself for priests, especially during her long drawn-out death agony which resembled that of St. Catherine. On the Friday before her death the Stigmata did not bleed, but the Lord conformed her to Himself by a lonely and abandoned death.

Together with St. Bernadette, the Curé d'Ars, Charles de Foucauld and others Louise Lateau, the stigmatic of Bois-d'Haine, preached, or rather lived, the message of the Cross before a world whose charity had grown cold. The wounds of St. Francis and his poverty were once more opposed to an age that hated both, whose gods were money and the body. But neither the Stigmata nor the material poverty are the whole story of this life. These extraordinary external manifestations were intimately bound up with the inner life of this soul who followed her Lord to the abandonment and the poverty of the Cross. The deeply hidden source of her holiness was a complete abandonment to the Will of God, expressed in six sayings which she had made the maxims of her life : " O Holy Will of God, you are my only happiness. My God, give me the grace to suffer in all things rather than fail in doing Thy Holy Will. God is love, justice and truth. To love God, it is necessary to speak the truth, and not to fear men. Everything passes, God alone remains. As God wills." Without this interior conformity to the Will of God the external conformity of the body would be a fraud. But where both are joined together, there is the true image of Christ held up to the world in a visible form, to proclaim in its own extraordinary way the mystery of Calvary and of its image on Mount Alvernia, to kindle new fires of the love of God in a materialistic age.

CHAPTER IV

TWO LOVERS OF THE SACRED HEART

St. Gertrude

Amor meus continuus,
Tibi languor assiduus,
Amor tuus suavissimus,
Mihi sapor gratissimus.
OUR LORD TO ST. GERTRUDE.

MODERN devotion to the Sacred Heart is closely associated with the name of St. Margaret Mary and popular practices such as the Nine Fridays and the Holy Hour, but its beginnings are not so well known. Yet it originated not at Paray-le-Monial but in the centres of medieval contemplative life, especially in the Benedictine, Cistercian and Carthusian monasteries. St. Gertrude, the famous mystic of Helfta, is perhaps its most striking representative.

Little is known of her outward life, which is not surprising, for she entered her convent at the age of five, never to leave it. She was born on the feast of the Epiphany, which unites so intimately liturgical splendour with mystic symbolism, as if to foreshadow the close union of both in her life, and gold, myrrh and incense abound in her visions. For at Helfta she grew up in the atmosphere of the slow, contemplative chant of the Divine Office and the dignified ceremonies of the Conventual Mass. As Dom Maurus Wolter so fittingly expresses it in his *Gertrudenbuch* : " St. Gertrude was a daughter of the cloister, Officium and Sacrificium, the Scripture and the Liturgy, are the two wings by which pure souls fly to God in the monastic life."

Yet we know from her *Legatus Divinæ Pietatis* that her early life, from her fifth to her twenty-fifth year, was spent chiefly in the pursuit of learning rather than in contemplative prayer. She was of unusual intelligence, knew Latin well, and was particularly interested in the Liberal Arts. But one Advent, probably in 1280, her hitherto peaceful life suddenly became troubled by a strange restlessness and an inexplicable feeling of interior emptiness. This state continued until the Monday before the Feast of the Purification, when, while she was standing in the dormitory after Compline, Our Lord appeared to her and placed His hand in hers saying : "I will save and deliver you, fear nothing. With my enemies you have licked the dust and looked for honey among the thorns. Return now, I will accept you and inebriate you with the streams of my Divine joy." From that time she abandoned her former interests and gave herself completely to prayer and the study of Scripture and the Fathers, especially St. Augustine, St. Gregory the Great, St. Bernard and Hugh of St. Victor, and she received the gift of instructing others in the mysteries of the faith. At the same time her inner life became a succession of the highest spiritual experiences, centred in the Humanity of Our Lord, which made her the mystic *par excellence* of the Incarnation and of the Sacred Heart. Henceforth she lives in the world of Divine charity, in which the smallest action radiates the love of the Divine Heart, and both the joys and the sufferings of earthly life are transfigured and made fruitful by the action of grace.

The centre of this newly developed mystical life is the Mass. Many of St. Gertrude's ecstasies occurred during it, and she is always careful to give the particular words which called forth her raptures. Thus at the Mass " *Gaudete* " of the Third Sunday in Advent her heart was pierced with an arrow of love—obviously an experience similar to St. Teresa's famous "Transverberation"— and on the Fourth Sunday of Lent, at the reading of the Gospel of the Feeding of the Five Thousand, Our Lord gave her five fishes with which to make a mystical offering to supply for the deficiencies of the Church. One of the most extraordinary graces was granted her on the Second Sunday of Lent, which has the Gospel of the Transfiguration. " It appeared to me," she writes, " that my face was pressed to another face. In this vision, Thine eyes, bright as the rays of the sun, appeared before mine, and when Thou didst show me Thy most adorable Face, a light of ineffable sweetness passed from Thy Divine eyes into mine, and thence into my inmost being."

Thus the Mass offers both the setting and the contents of her contemplation : the Holy Spirit guides, as it were, her imagination along the lines traced out in the Liturgy, to which the Divine action adapts itself in her soul. This is even more obvious in the great visions in which, while the ordinary Mass is going on in the church, St. Gertrude, rapt in ecstasy, assists at a mystical Mass offered by Our Lord Himself in Heaven. In an extraordinary interplay of liturgical and mystical worship, both deeply penetrating each other, she describes the liturgical actions performed in Heaven down to their minutest details and fills them with mystical significance, using to the full those mysterious faculties known in mystic theology as the " spiritual senses." Sight and hearing, smelling, touch and taste are all transformed, and those God-given senses of the body, which the Church elevates and satisfies in her worship, are reproduced in an incorporeal manner in the purified soul of the contemplative to enable her to take part in what is above the capacities of ordinary Christians.

One of the most perfect examples of this close relation between the mystical and the liturgical life is her magnificent vision at the Matins of the Assumption. From the Most Holy Trinity down to the lowest choirs of angels the whole court of Heaven combines to pay honour to the Blessed Virgin on her greatest feast. The Holy Spirit chants : " *Una est columba mea* " ; the Divine Son responds " *Perfecta mea*," and the Eternal Father Himself concludes : "*Una est matris suæ electa*." Thus the Office continues, the Divine Trinity and Our Lord in His humanity, angels and Saints chanting together, until at last Our Lady herself sings the *Te Deum* in thanksgiving for the Divine condescension that made her the Mother of God. Here is, indeed, realised the unity of the human life, the participation of the whole man in his highest act, which is worship.

It is, therefore, not surprising, that the central devotion of her life, too, should be intimately linked up with the Liturgy. Like St. Margaret Mary, she receives the great revelation of the Sacred Heart on the Feast of St. John, not, however, as the modern Saint at the time of private prayer, but at Matins. The Apostle appears to her and invites her to come with him, that they may rest together on the Breast of the Lord. Then, taking her up with him, he presents her to Jesus and places her on His right side, reposing himself on the left. This he does, as he explains, so that she may drink more easily the consolations flowing from His Divine Heart, for it was the right side that was pierced by the lance. Then, as the beating of the Divine Heart fills her with ineffable joy, she asks St. John why he had written nothing about it in his Gospel, and he replies : " It was my mission to instruct the Church in her earliest age in the mysteries of the Uncreated Word, so far as they may be comprehended. But I did not speak about the sweetness of the

Divine Heart-beats until these later ages, so that the world that has grown cold may be rekindled by the knowledge of these mysteries."

There is a striking difference between the Sacred Heart as revealed to St. Gertrude and the great visions of St. Margaret Mary. In the life of the modern Saint the Sacred Heart is almost always seen in sufferings, despised by men, asking for love and reparation. We are in the world of the great apostasy which began in the sixteenth century and still continues, imparting to our whole life as Christians a spirit of martyrdom, as it were, that is poignantly conscious of the forces of evil around us. St. Gertrude, it is true, also preaches the necessity of suffering and reparation but it is a reparation for sinners within the fold of the One Church, within a Europe in which Christianity and civilisation are still synonyms. There the Sacred Heart shows itself radiant in glory, loving and beloved, and the mystic responds joyfully, singing " a canticle on the instrument of thy Divine Heart by the virtue of the Spirit of consolation." The whole spiritual life of St. Gertrude, dominated as it is by her close union with the Sacred Heart, breathes an extraordinary happiness. The Heart of Jesus is a treasure house in which are enclosed all riches, it is a lyre moved by the Holy Ghost, a golden censer from which ascend sweet-smelling perfumes, or a lamp suspended between Heaven and earth. The Divine Heart is, as its were, her home to which she is called by the Voice of her Heavenly Lover : *Veni, mea, ad me ! Intra, meum, in me !* He frequently draws her into His Heart during contemplation, and this close union produces a delightful intimacy between the Creator and one of His most favoured creatures. This intimacy may even occasionally shock the modern reader, as when the Saint asks Our Lord all manner of questions, desiring detailed explanations of His actions. We are so very grown-up that we have almost forgotten that the prayer Our Lord Himself taught us really means to come to Him as children to their Father, though He made it so unmistakably clear that this is the only attitude acceptable to Him. St. Gertrude had this attitude, and the example of her, who was a woman of great intelligence and learning, may serve to dissipate the prejudice as if the childlike mind required by Our Lord were incompatible with high intellectual gifts—a combination, by the way, not unknown in the greatest Doctors of the Church.

This childlike trust in God's fatherly goodness penetrates

Gertrude's whole life, and reveals itself especially in her relation to the Blessed Sacrament, so much less approached in her time than in our own. It seems as if devotion to the Sacred Heart necessarily entails the desire for frequent Communion, of which the Saint was one of the most ardent advocates. When she is full of anxiety on account of her unworthiness Our Lord Himself quietens her fears : " He who communicates from a pure desire of my glory never communicates irreverently" He tells her. And of one of her Sisters who abstained from fear He said : " What can I do for her, since she herself has so covered her eyes with the veil of her unworthiness that she cannot see the tenderness of my paternal Heart ? "

But this tenderness which the Saint extols is very far from soft-ness. For the close relation between the Divine Heart and the mystic is based on the perfect conformity of her will to the Will of God and on her profound humility. " When she humbled herself at the remembrance of her faults, Our Lord poured forth on her from His Sacred Heart all the virtue and beauty of His Divine perfections." It may be called an unalterable law of the spiritual life that the humility of man calls forth the gifts of God, and that the progressive giving-up of one's own will is invariably answered by an ever-more perfect indwelling of God in the soul. This surrender of man's will must embrace even the most legitimate and holy desires of the soul. Thus Our Lord shows Himself dis-pleased when St. Gertrude asks Him to restore her health so that she may again follow her Rule : for He wants her to practise the greater perfection of complete abandonment to Divine Providence. Here she touches the theme that will be so fully orchestrated by St. John of the Cross three centuries later : " I know," says Our Lord to her, " that if I grant what you ask and allow you to assist at these services, I shall be obliged to follow you into the place which pleases you ; whereas, if I refuse you this, and you still continue patient, you will follow me into the place which I prefer. For I am better pleased with your good intentions in a state of suffering than with the sweetness of your devotion that gives pleasure to yourself."

Thus St. Gertrude, in all the joys of her contemplation, knows the fundamental truth of the mystic life, that the giving up of our own will, however pious its aspirations, is the one great condition of union with God. When she asks Our Lord why He so often

deprives souls of spiritual consolation on feast days or at the moment
of Holy Communion, He replies that He prefers good intentions
and humility to sensible devotion, and she is reminded that " sufferings of body and mind are proofs of the spiritual espousals of God
and the soul." Despite all the extraordinary graces showered on
her, she is often overwhelmed with sadness, and never ceases to
bewail the enormity of her faults. It is one of the greatest puzzles
to many Christians how the Saints, in the midst of all the graces
given to them, can preserve such genuine humility which is unattainable to those who would seem to have so much more reason
for it. This is one of the paradoxes of the spiritual life, but St.
Gertrude gives a key to it when she records Our Lord's words :
" My graces usually serve to humble you, because you think
yourself unworthy of them." There is a parallel even in the natural
sphere. When a man and a woman truly love each other, each
will think that the other is far superior, and the more marks of
love they receive from one another, the less will they believe
themselves to deserve them. . . . Now if that happens in the
human sphere, how much more in the love of the creature for its
Creator, between whom there is an infinite distance, which can
only be bridged by the ineffable condescension of the Beloved.
Thus in the mystic life, which is the life of love at its highest,
humility grows apace with love, for there is no real love apart
from it, and St. Paul's great canticle of charity is at the same time
the most beautiful hymn to humility.

This humility, given to St. Gertrude to defend her from her
human frailty, enables her to receive all those high graces which
flow from the Divine Heart. Visions and revelations succeed one
another, Our Lord, Our Lady and the Saints speak to her as familiarly
as her sisters, but, despite this distinctly visionary spirituality, a
type which so often leads to vagaries of the imagination, its close
connection with the Liturgy safeguards the doctrinal correctness
of her revelations. In her the words of the Mass or of the Office,
under the action of the Holy Ghost, call forth the scenes which she
witnesses. Her mysticism, however personal, is always carried
by the action of the Church, which gives it its singular attraction,
comparable to that of the colourful yet austere paintings of the
Middle Ages. On the other hand, her close connection with the
supernatural world imparts to her an admirable wisdom, which
people of all conditions come to consult. Her rules of conduct,

scattered throughout her writings, show that she possessed the virtue of prudence and the gift of counsel in an eminent degree. When she is doubtful whether some revelations come from God she is given this rule for the discernment of spirits : " Whoever knows in his heart that his will is so united to mine as never to dissent from it, whether in prosperity or adversity, and who acts and suffers in all things only for my glory, may surely believe that what he learns interiorly is from me, if it is useful to others and not opposed to the Scriptures." We have here, as in the teaching of all genuine mystics, once more the one and only safe rule : " By their fruits you shall know them." False mystics place their confidence in extraordinary states, complete passivity, feelings of delectation and even the conviction that their strange experiences have rendered them impeccable. True mystics seek only the glory of God and the edification of their neighbour, for mystic prayer progressively reduces self, and the mystic, like St. John Baptist, knows that he must decrease so that Jesus may increase until the soul has attained to the stature of Christ.

This growth of God in the soul, so often accompanied by storms and crises, seems to have taken place in the soul of St. Gertrude with singular tranquillity. In her life there is no tension, no incongruity between the heavenly world and her earthly surroundings, which, on the contrary, seem to interpenetrate each other, and the rich brocades and precious stones, in which her visions and allegories abound, are as perfectly suited to this monastic mysticism as to the tender Virgins and Saints of Fra Angelico. Nature and supernature are blended into an harmonious whole in the soul of this Benedictine nun, to whom Our Lord said that he uses sensible things to make men understand the supra-sensible mysteries, " therefore no one should esteem spiritual things less because they are hidden under corporeal images."

This teaching is certainly in full accord with the Angelic Doctor's insistence that all our knowledge comes to us by the mediation of our senses—but does it not perhaps contradict St. John of the Cross, who constantly warns beginners to distrust visions and locutions ? But then St. John of the Cross was himself a Thomist, and his vigorous expressions, called forth by very real dangers, must not be interpreted in a one-sided manner. The great Doctor of mysticism knew well that these experiences have their legitimate place in the contemplative life. But they can become a fatal hindrance, if they are coveted for their own sake, for the satisfaction of pride and from "spiritual gluttony," not however when they are humbly received as marks of undeserved Divine favour and as means of instruction used in the service of charity and submitted to authority. For though the *gratiæ gratum facientes* are the only ones we are allowed to desire for ourselves, yet it would be ungrateful, indeed, to belittle those *gratiæ gratis datæ* given to the Saints to strengthen our faith and inflame our love. They, like all other graces, flow from the inexhaustible source of grace, the Divine Heart, which Our Lord showed to St. Gertrude under the image of a burning lamp : "Behold, I present to the eyes of your soul my loving Heart, the organ of the Holy Trinity, that it may accomplish in you all the good that you cannot perform yourself." This Heart, through which the Holy Trinity works in our hearts, will one day make itself known to all Christians in the darkness of strife and heresy—no longer radiant in glory, but sorrowful even unto death, asking for reparation in a world that has abandoned the worship of God for the worship of man.

St. Margaret Mary

WHEN St. Gertrude asked St. John during her great vision on his Feast why he had written nothing about the Sacred Heart in his Gospel, he replied that these secrets of Love were reserved "until these later ages, so that the world that has grown cold may be rekindled by the knowledge of these mysteries." If we repeat her question, wishing to know why devotion to the Divine Heart of Our Lord had remained the unknown possession of the chosen few until the end of the seventeenth century, we should probably receive the same answer. When Love had grown quite cold, when the country of St. Gertrude was ravaged by heresy and religious wars, when England seemed to be lost to the Faith for ever, when the Eldest Daughter of the Church gloried in the reign of the debauched Roi Soleil, and when the first pale rays of the "Enlightenment" appeared on the horizon of Europe, the time was come for the Lord to reveal His Heart, to oppose to the cold artificial light of Rationalism the burning fire of His Love.

He did it in His own way, the way that will ever be "to the

Jews a stumbling block and to the Greeks foolishness." This time He revealed Himself not to a cultivated Benedictine, living a life devoted to scholarship in a monastery resplendent with the glory of art and of the Liturgy. That would have been too little in the spirit of the contradiction of the Cross. No. He took a little French bourgeoise, devout but not averse to the amusements of ordinary life, placed her in the obscurest little convent of the most hidden contemplative Order of the Church and required from her to be the Victim of His Heart. And so little Sister Margaret Mary Alacoque, whose surname was to become a source of sarcastic mirth to her renowned countryman Voltaire, began to have ecstasies and revelations at which her whole Convent looked askance, and finally established a new devotion in the Universal Church. Surely, if human prudence had been asked to name an unlikely person for such a task it might have named Soeur Alacoque.

But the Lord's ways are not our ways, and He who confounds the mighty and the worldly-wise knew how to prepare His chosen instrument. It seems as if Divine Providence had meant to indicate the difference in the vocation of the two great lovers of the Sacred Heart even in the choice of their birthdays. For St. Gertrude came into the world on the radiant Feast of the Epiphany, but St. Margaret Mary was born on the day of St. Mary Magdalen, the Saint of rude penance and contemplation. Her life and mission are unintelligible unless we see in her the mystic of reparation, whose whole spirituality was built on the foundation of penitential suffering. Even as a child she was compelled by a mysterious power, much against her natural inclinations, to abandon the games and pleasures of her little friends to seek a hidden corner where to pray, and at the age of four she was inspired to make a vow of virginity, before she could know even the meaning of the words. And when she grew up into an attractive young woman, there was that force again, drawing her away from ordinary occupations by strange illnesses, which the doctors knew not how to treat, and during which she could neither walk nor eat nor sleep. And then she was suddenly cured—after making a vow to consecrate herself entirely to Our Lady. She now gave herself up to a life of prayer and intense mortification, sleeping on the bare ground and disciplining herself with chains.

But nature was not to give in to the spirit without a struggle.

As in the lives of many women Saints, St. Catherine of Siena and St. Teresa for example, the superhuman effort of the soul was followed by a reaction. There is, perhaps, no more decisive moment in the natural life of woman than when she first realizes her power to please men. It is a power closely linked to one of the two deepest instincts implanted by God in human nature, the instinct for the propagation of the race. And, like all the natural powers of man, it can be used in three ways : it may be abused— as Adam abused free will—or it may be used for the purpose for which it was given, or, in response to a Divine call, it may be renounced for the sake of a greater good and by that very renunciation be transformed into something higher : the desire to be pleasing to God alone, to adorn not the body for an earthly lover, but the soul for the great Lover of souls. When this call comes there must necessarily be a struggle ; and sometimes this struggle against a legitimate instinct may be far more painful than the struggle against sin, precisely because the instinct is not wrong in itself— so St. Francis de Sales told Ste. Chantal to let her marriageable daughter dress attractively so as not to repel acceptable suitors by a misplaced austerity.

Margaret Mary knew in her heart of hearts that she was never meant to marry—yet there were young men frequenting her house, there was her mother imploring her to choose a husband so that she could make her home with her ; there were all her friends and even priests urging her to give in to her mother's wish—and, most powerful of all, there was her own natural desire for ordinary womanly happiness. Yet there was another Voice. There was her vow—though she knew well that there would be no difficulty about that—perhaps not even a dispensation would be necessary, seeing that she had not reached the age of discretion when she made it. Still, the voice persisted. She tried to quieten it by redoubling her penances—if she disciplined herself unto blood, surely the Lord would be satisfied with that ? But the blood that is shed from self-will is no more pleasing to Him than the blood of bulls and goats. He appeared to her one day as He was after the Scourging reproaching her for her infidelity—but she still struggled against the Call. At last Grace touched her in the depths. One morning after Holy Communion, the Lord moved the will of His creature and she submitted.

From now on extraordinary graces multiply. She is guided

interiorly to the Visitation—the very Order most opposed to anything extraordinary. From the day of her Clothing which, Our Lord told her, was her spiritual Betrothal, the interior favours she received begin to be manifested outwardly. Her superiors are alarmed. They reproach her severely, telling her that such things are contrary to the spirit of the Institute, that she cannot be admitted to profession if she continues to have these states of absorption. So they give her the most distracting occupations in the novitiate and cut down her time of prayer. What can she do ?

> " Plus l'on contredit mon amour,
> Plus cet unique bien m'enflamme.
> Que l'on m'afflige nuit et jour,
> On ne peut l'ôter à mon âme.
> Oui, plus je souffre de douleur,
> Plus mon Dieu s'unit à mon coeur."

Even human passion thrives on contradiction, how much more Divine Love, sealed with the Cross. When she was at last allowed to make her Profession Retreat Our Lord told her that henceforth there would be no pleasure for her that would not be overshadowed by His Cross. "To love and to suffer blindly" became her watchword.

For Margaret Mary was what is to-day called a "victim soul." It is difficult to appreciate rightly this victim state. Not only is it opposed to the general temper of our age with its particular dread of physical pain, but the very word "victim" has an unpleasant ring about it—suggesting weakness, passivity, helpless yielding to superior force, as it is used in the newspapers for "victims of the Nazis," or "victims of a 'flu epidemic." But when we go back to its original Christian sense, as it comes out for example in the glorious Paschal Sequence *Victimæ paschali*, it becomes charged with a different meaning. The victim is no longer a helpless creature tormented against his will, but the *Sanctus Fortis*, willingly offering His Body to torture and death for the salvation of many. It is no longer passive, but supremely active, exercising the virtue of obedience with the full force of a human will united to the Divine. And the self-giving of the victim was completed when His Side was opened on the Cross and the lance wounded His Heart, thus offering Itself to the Father in reparation for the hardness of the hearts of men.

As the Divine Heart was a victim of reparation for human sin, so Margaret Mary, whom Our Lord called the Disciple of His Sacred Heart, was to follow her Master in this office. By becoming the " Victim of His Heart " she abandoned all her natural desires for happiness, esteem and the rest, by an ever-to-be-renewed self-giving, possible only to a strong will acting under the powerful impulse of grace. This, then, was to be her life as a professed nun of the Visitation. It was a very special vocation, and so we must not be surprised if the element of joy, so characteristic of most Saints, is, if not exactly absent, at least so much modified in her as to take on an altogether different character.

From the day of her Profession she began to be conscious of Our Lord's Presence in a new manner. She felt Him as if He were constantly near her, and this feeling caused her the most profound abjection, expressing itself even in her outward attitude, for whenever she was alone she was either prostrate on the ground or on her knees. Our Lord told her that the more she would retire into her own nothingness, the more would He condescend to her. He kept His promise with Divine generosity ; for in the year following her profession she had the first of the great Revelations of the Sacred Heart. Like St. Gertrude, she received it on the Feast of St. John, and like her she was allowed to rest for several hours on the Sacred Breast of Our Lord. Then He opened His Heart to her, all inflamed with love for men, and told her that He had chosen her " as an abyss of unworthiness and ignorance " to reveal It to the world. He took her heart from her, placed it within His own, and, withdrawing it as a tiny heart-shaped flame of fire, restored it to its place. From that day she often had agonising pains in her side, especially on Fridays, which could be relieved only by bleeding. Nor was this the only suffering attached to the overwhelming favour. Her Sisters refused to believe either in her revelations or in her pains and treated her as a visionary and a *malade imaginaire*.

Ever since St. Paul was afflicted with his mysterious " thorn in the flesh " lest the greatness of the revelations should exalt him, the mystics have had to endure the most bitter humiliations, particularly in the beginning of their ecstatic life. For Divine Love knows the weakness of the fallen race. Before St. Catherine could safely have her hands kissed by the enthusiastic populace she had to be thrown on the dustheap in her ecstasies ; ere Teresa of Jesus was asked for her blessing by a bishop she was maligned as a restless gadabout full of illusions. Thus, with each new revelation, St. Margaret Mary's conflicts increased. One day during the Octave of Corpus Christi, probably in 1674, while the Blessed Sacrament was exposed, Our Lord appeared to her "all resplendent in glory, His Five Wounds shining like five suns, His Heart on fire in His open Breast." He complained at the cold neglect with which men repayed His ardent love and asked her to make reparation. Every First Friday of the month He desires her to receive Holy Communion, and every Thursday, from eleven to twelve at night, she is to keep vigil prostrate on the ground, in honour of His agony in the Garden. She went to her Superior, Mère de Saumaise, and told her what she had been ordered to do, with the result that she was forbidden to carry out anything Our Lord had commanded her. She obeyed—but she suffered deeply, both spiritually and physically. So she fulfilled the designs of the Holy Trinity once shown her in a vision, in which the Father presented her with a Cross studded with thorns, Our Lord told her that He would attach her to it, and the Holy Ghost promised to purify and consume her on it.

But Mère de Saumaise was troubled about this strange daughter of hers, so gentle and obedient as a lamb, yet always having visions, revelations and incomprehensible illnesses which would vanish suddenly at the Mother's request for a sign. So she called in some theologians, and Margaret Mary had to undergo the ordeal of telling them exactly what passed between her and her Lord. The theologians cried "illusion," condemned her attraction for prayer, and forbade her to follow her inspirations. The Holy Ghost was indeed doing His work of purification by the contradictions of creatures, and so the Lord's designs were fulfilled, though to human eyes they would seem to be frustrated.

Relief came when a young Jesuit, Père de la Colombière, came to Paray and undertook her direction. He told her to abandon herself completely to the will of God in order to be immolated according to His good pleasure. She needed this support, for she was soon to receive another revelation with orders that concerned not only herself, but the whole Church. Once more it was the Octave of Corpus Christi (1675), once more she was shown the Sacred Heart. "Behold this Heart, which has so loved man. . ." The Divine Love, exposed on the altars in the Blessed Sacrament, received but blasphemies and insults in return for Its condescension. Therefore a Feast of the Sacred Heart was to be instituted on the Friday following the Octave of Corpus Christi. Margaret Mary was dismayed. How should she, a poor enclosed nun, institute a new Feast in the Church ? She was told that Père de la Colombière would help her.

From that time her whole life was given to the propagation of the new devotion. Her conversation, her correspondence, all her thoughts were directed to this one end. There were practices in honour of the Sacred Heart to be recommended, pictures to be drawn, letters to be written, altars and oratories to be decorated. We seem to be very far from the serene calm of the mystic devotion of Helfta. Yet the mystic life of St. Margaret Mary was as genuine as that of St. Gertrude. But their vocations were different. To St. Gertrude the Sacred Heart was revealed for her own delight and progress in perfection, to St. Margaret Mary for the sake of others. She was in the fullest sense called to "*contemplata aliis tradere.*" For this reason suffering held such a much larger place in her life than in that of the medieval Saint. The Apostle is always a martyr, whether physically or spiritually, and the less strenuous external activity is involved in his apostolate, the greater is the interior martyrdom, though it may consist only of seemingly trivial renunciations, as for example in the case of Ste. Thérèse de Lisieux and of St. Margaret Mary herself.

To a mind nurtured on the atrocities of modern warfare and dictatorships the sufferings of an enclosed religious may perhaps appear very slight. Our world, blinded as it is to all but the physical aspects of things, can understand suffering only in terms of physical pain. Yet it is the teaching of all the mystics that the keenest physical suffering, though it may be such as to reduce the soul to complete inactivity, cannot be compared to the horrors of the "Night of the Spirit." Nor were they unaware of what they were talking about ; they were all subject to long and painful illnesses, and St. John of the Cross's imprisonment at Toledo for instance must have resembled modern concentration camps pretty closely. Moreover, the higher the development of the spiritual organism, the keener its sensibility—the mystics' capacity for suffering seems to grow proportionately as their contemplation advances. And, lastly, the possibilities of suffering are enhanced to an extraordinary degree in a strictly enclosed community, where the smallest event, even a word or a gesture, will produce far deeper reactions than in a life with ordinary outside influences and distractions.

Two years after the last great revelation Our Lord commanded Margaret Mary to inform the community that she was to be the victim for the expiation of their sins. As a result of this extraordinary message she was regarded as possessed by the devil and her sisters threw Holy Water at her when they met her. For a long time afterwards she could hardly eat or sleep, feeling only " a sink of abjection." Soon afterwards she was afflicted with strange temptations to " gluttony," suffering violent fits of hunger during prayer time, and as violent an aversion against all food the moment she entered the refectory. At other times she was tempted to despair, tortured by the fear of being deluded. The offices given her in the Community were extremely distasteful to her, though when she was novice mistress, she had great opportunities of promoting her beloved devotion. It was plain to herself that this constant suffering, even under occupations that should normally have brought her some satisfaction, must have a supernatural origin. " He willed," she wrote, "that I should be in a continual state of sacrifice, and therefore He told me that He would increase my sensibility and repugnance to such a degree that I should be unable to do anything without trouble and violence." Once more, hers was a very special vocation to a life of constant immolation, as she herself wrote : " I only find true happiness in crosses, contempt and suffering."

It is this unmistakable sign of the Cross with which her life is marked that is the surest proof of the authenticity of her mysticism and of her mission. As she was constantly afraid of illusion Our Lord once told her by which signs to recognize Him. His graces, He said, would always be accompanied by some humiliation or contradiction ; they would be followed by confusion and a feeling of annihilation ; moreover, they would never cause her to despise others, nor would they prevent her from following her Rule. Finally, they would result in a great love of Himself, in a perfect imitation of His example, in the desire to suffer for His sake, but to suffer unobserved, and in an unquenchable thirst for Holy Communion and for being near the Blessed Sacrament. Margaret Mary spent almost every free moment before the Tabernacle. For devotion to the Sacred Heart seems to be inseparably linked to an ardent love for the Blessed Sacrament. All the practices in honour of the Sacred Heart, the First Friday Communion, the Holy Hour, the Feast itself, after the Octave of Corpus Christi, they all are at the same time devotions to the Blessed Sacrament. The great visions of St. Gertrude and of St. Margaret Mary both took place on the Feast of St. John the disciple who rested on the Breast of Jesus during the Last Supper, when He instituted the Eucharist, and both visions are, in a way, reproductions of that scene. St. Margaret Mary's mysticism is, therefore, in a very real sense, a sacramental mysticism, centred in the hidden life of Jesus in the Host. And as the Blessed Sacrament is pre-eminently the Sacrament of Love, so the Sacred Heart is the visible sign of this Love, the Heart of flesh, which is the seat of life and whose beating registers the emotions of the soul.

The great mystics have usually a mission in the history of the Church. St. Bernard, St. Catherine, St. Teresa—they appeared at the exact moment when their work and influence was needed, though its full significance was only discovered by posterity. St. Margaret Mary, too, had an historical mission. The Sacred Heart was revealed to her at the same time as France was in the throes of Jansenism. The hard cold creed of Jansenius and Saint-Cyran set up an all but unattainable ideal of sanctity as a condition for the reception of Holy Communion, and in their zeal for the incomparable holiness and transcendence of God they almost forgot that He is also Love. The very form of their crucifixes, with arms stretched high over the head, indicated that the Redeemer Himself was unapproachable. Jansenism had powerful adherents, of high intellectual qualities, such as Pascal, and great personal holiness, as many of the nuns and hermits of Port Royal. But its influence was disastrous, for it kept the people away from the Sacraments, the main source of holiness. It was St. Margaret Mary's mission to proclaim the condescending Love of God by showing to the world His Sacred Heart. The God who was made Man in Jesus was not a fear-inspiring despot whom no one dared approach, but a God of Love, who, showing to man His human Heart hypostatically united to His Divinity, invited them to come to Him lovingly, without fear, like children to their Father. It was devotion to the Sacred Heart which gradually uprooted Jansenism, which had found a very firm foothold especially in France and Belgium ; it was the sufferings and humility of St. Margaret Mary that overcame the force of heresy and finally obtained the consecration of all mankind to the Sacred Heart (Leo XIII in 1899). For the works of God follow always the same Law : they start with the smallest, most insignificant beginnings ; they are contradicted, ridiculed and persecuted, and finally they triumph. The grain of mustard seed sown in the soul of a poor nun at Paray-le-Monial has become a large tree, spreading over the whole world, for wherever the Church is the Sacred Heart is known and loved. The Sacred Heart is loved—but St. Margaret Mary has almost disappeared, as St. Bernardette disappeared behind Our Lady. That, too, is as she would have wished it to be, for her life, as that of every true mystic, was centred not in her own heart, but in the Heart of her God.

CHAPTER V

Two Founders of Contemplative Orders

St. Teresa

The time of the Counter-Reformation was a period filled with feverish activity. The Church had sustained heavy losses, but with the supernatural vitality of its life the old tree brought forth new branches everywhere. The greatest and most conspicuous of them was the Society of Jesus, the new Order in which the obligations of Divine Office and mental prayer were restricted to a minimum so as to leave its members as free as possible for apostolic action. But the Church, like the human body, is an admirably balanced organism in which the strength it gives out must be constantly replaced. What food and sleep are to the individual body, contemplation is to the Church ; without the spiritual strength accumulated by her contemplatives her active members would be left without their most efficacious support ; for the household in which Our Lord takes His delight needs both Martha to serve and Mary to rest at His Feet.

When St. Ignatius founded his Society most of the contemplative Orders had long fallen from their first fervour, and nuns who should have drawn down graces on the world by their prayers and mortifications spent their time chattering in the parlours and carrying on silly intrigues. When St. Teresa, after a heart-breaking wrench from the world which she loved, entered the Carmelite Convent of the Incarnation at Avila (1536) this was the life she found there. But she had not come to the cloister to live at her ease, and in her youthful fervour she began at once to carry her desire for sanctity and self-sacrifice beyond the limits of her endurance. After eighteen months at the convent there came a grave crisis, expressing itself in physical disorders as well as mental distress. She was sent home, and the long illness that followed left its traces in violent headaches and fits of vomiting for the rest of her life. But in the agonies of this mysterious disease, on the nature of which doctors still speculate, she learned a lesson needed

H

above all others by the future foundress of an austere contemplative Order. Never afterwards did she attempt to go beyond her physical strength in the pursuit of sanctity, nor did she impose on others burdens they were unable to bear.

She had been initiated into the mystery of suffering, the twin sister of contemplation here on earth ; but the time for her to become one of the greatest mystics of the Church was not yet. She returned to her convent in 1538, and for the next seventeen years led the life of an exemplary nun of the Mitigated Observance, keeping her easy Rule, frequenting the parlour where she was much in demand because of her charm and wit, and differing little from the more fervent among her Sisters except for her great charity that could not suffer to hear anyone ill-spoken of. Her prayer during all these years was arid and painful, and despite all her friendships—or perhaps rather because of them—her life seemed empty and without a purpose. She was forty, an age at which normally the best years of a woman are spent, when the life for which God had created her began.

A few months after reading the stirring account of St. Augustine's conversion in his *Confessions* which had deeply impressed her, she found herself praying before a statue of Christ bound to the pillar. It was one of those moments of grace when the Creator deigns to act immediately on the will of His creature and impart to its life a new direction. When Teresa came out of the oratory there was only one way left to her to tread, the "Way of Perfection," which is the way of love as it is the way of abnegation.

Love had caught her, and now she wanted nothing but to immerse herself in this Love and to draw ever nearer to the Divine Lover. It is thus also that human love begins : a glance, a word, and the fire is kindled, and the lover wants to be alone with the beloved. But once the marriage is consummated, the lovers will remain not long alone, for all love is meant to bear fruit. When the honeymoon is over, work has to be done : the family grows and the first transports are forgotten. But love throws its roots ever more deeply into the soul, and, purified by sorrows and trials borne in common, becomes that steady union which sometimes results even in the assimilation of the physical features of husband and wife. Thus Divine Love, too, normally develops slowly, growing in intensity and steadiness, and St. Teresa is still unsurpassed in the lucid description of these successive stages on the way to the Mystic Life.

She lays the foundations very deep, building the lofty edifice of the Interior Castle on the rocks of humility and detachment from creatures, a detachment that is " not won by removing the body, but by the determination of the soul to embrace the good Jesus, Our Lord, to find everything in Him and to forget all else." For all our ills, she insists, come to us because we do not keep our eyes fixed on Him. If we would only regard Him who called Himself the Way, we should soon arrive at our journey's end. But He gave Himself as our model above all because He was " meek and humble of heart." For " humility," she says," is the foundation of the whole building, and unless you are truly humble, Our Lord, for your sake, will never permit you to rear it very high, lest it should fall to the ground." As the standard bearer in battle carries the flag, " so ought contemplatives to bear aloft the flag of humility, and to suffer whatever blows are given them, without retaliating." Where true humility exists, even should God never grant consolations, " yet He gives a peace and resignation which make the soul happier than are others with sensible devotion." It is the want of humility that stops progress in prayer, of a humility carried to a point which, without the most faithful co-operation with grace, no man can hope to attain here on earth, for " not only should we wish others to consider us the worst of all ; we should strive to make them think so." It is as though humility were a shadow cast by the sublime light of contemplation to temper its brilliancy and prevent its hurting the creature not yet established in the glory of the Beatific Vision. True humility is the prerequisite of contemplation, but at the same time it grows in proportion to the progress of contemplation, and the Queen of Contemplatives is also the *ancilla Domini* whose humility merited the Incarnation.

Yet even humility can be counterfeited and falsified. In Teresa's time contemplative prayer was regarded with suspicion ; it was deemed an extraordinary favour which it was dangerous to receive, let alone to desire. Humility, so it was thought, required even that it should be rejected. The Saint herself had to suffer grievously from directors who believed her to be subject to illusions, ordering her to give up her manner of prayer and to keep at a distance the Lord who desires nothing so much as that He should be loved by

His creatures. Therefore she repeatedly warns her daughters not to listen to such advisers. " Leave aside," she tells them," a certain reserve, which some people keep up, thinking it is humility. But humility is not shown by refusing a favour which the King does us, but rather by accepting it, recognizing that it comes to us un-merited, and rejoicing in it—Banish, daughters, this false humility, and treat with Him as with a Father, a Brother, a Master, and a Lover."

It was thus that He taught Teresa to treat with Him, once the sight of Him, scourged and bleeding at the pillar, had inflamed her with love. This is the reason, too, why she passes so quickly through the first three " mansions " of her Interior Castle, occupied by meditation and the prayer of recollection, impatient, as it were, to arrive at the first stage of the mystic life, because it is the life of love. Until St. Teresa set herself to describe the ascent of the soul towards God, no spiritual writer had treated in detail of those intermediate stages of the mystic way which she calls the Prayer of Quiet and the Prayer of Union. Between the prayer of medita-tion practised by the majority of the devout and the ecstasies of the saints there was a region which so far no one had taken the trouble to investigate. But in the normal order of the interior life —though, of course, there are exceptions—the soul is raised to the state of ecstasy only after a prolonged sojourn in the inferior stages of contemplation. As these forms of mystic prayer are far less obvious than ecstasy they are much more difficult to analyze, and the admirable lucidity which the saint achieves in her de-scriptions can hardly be solely attributed to her remarkable psychological insight and her literary gifts. The depositions of her nuns who affirmed that she wrote with her face inflamed, frequently surrounded by an unearthly light and at an abnormal speed, would confirm the impression that she received super-natural aid in the writing of her books, those *cælestis sapientiæ documenta* as the Roman Breviary calls them.

Once St. Teresa had given herself wholly to a life of perfection God again bestowed on her the prayer of quiet and of union, granted to her in her first period of fervour, and then withheld for eighteen years of painful aridity and distractions. In the famous simile of the two basins, one filled laboriously by means of many pipes and waterworks, the other immediately from the spring, she develops the difference between the prayer of meditation and

the prayer of quiet.   For, unlike meditation, the prayer of quiet is
" a tranquillizing of the soul, which the Lord works by His
presence.   It seems to her that there is nothing left to desire :
her powers are at rest, they do not wish to stir : every movement
seems to hinder love," in short, " the soul is like a babe at
its mother's breast, who feeds it without its having to move its
lips."

But Teresa is never satisfied with descriptions only.   What
matters most to her, who has become the guide of innumerable
souls to perfection, is the effects of such prayer, without which it
would be sterile.   Those who receive these graces will be more
desirous to do penance than before, and more indifferent to
sufferings.   They should strive, moreover, to become completely
detached from everything, because else they would be at a stand-
still.   For those who have been raised to the state of Quiet should
aspire towards the Prayer of Union, for which an ever-increasing
detachment is needed.

This Prayer of Union is intimately connected with the Prayer
of Quiet, and according to St. Teresa there are very few contemplatives who, having reached the state of Quiet, are not from
time to time admitted to the Prayer of Union.   For this prayer
differs from the prayer of Quiet principally in degree.   It is far
more absorbing.   " In the prayer of union," says the Saint, " the
soul is asleep, fast asleep, as regards the world and itself : in fact,
during the short time this state lasts it is deprived of all feeling
whatever, being unable to think on any subject, even if it wished. . .
The mind entirely concentrates on trying to understand what is
happening, which is beyond its power ; it is so astounded that, if
consciousness is not completely lost, at least no movement is
possible."   Into this kind of prayer the devil cannot enter, and the
soul itself " neither sees, hears, nor understands anything while
this state lasts, which is never more than a very brief time."   Yet
" God visits the soul in a manner which prevents its doubting,
on returning to itself, that it dwelt in Him and that He was within
it, and so firmly is it convinced of this truth that, although years
may pass before this favour recurs, the soul can never forget it
nor doubt the fact."   Here, again, the genuineness of the experience
is best proved by its effects, which are that " the soul desires to
praise Our Lord God and longs to sacrifice itself and die a thousand
deaths for Him.   It feels an unconquerable desire for great crosses

and would like to perform the most severe penances ; it sighs for solitude and would have all men to know God."

St. Teresa herself, who corresponded to all the graces given her with the utmost fidelity, passed quickly through these first stages of mystic prayer, in which the majority of contemplatives would seem to remain all their lives. In her case they were accompanied by many accidental phenomena such as visions and especially locutions. In 1558, three years after her " conversion," she had her first rapture. From that time onwards she was almost overwhelmed with an outpouring of the most extraordinary graces. There is the famous transverberation of her heart through the fiery dart plunged into it by a seraph ; there are violent transports and frequent levitations, and there is, at the end of this ecstatic state, the celebrated ecstasy of Salamanca from which she came forth with the oft-quoted words : " I die for that I cannot die."

These ecstasies of the saints always make wonderful reading and we may sometimes ask ourselves what it must be like to live them. Once more St. Teresa is an excellent guide, so much the more because she reveals not only the sublimity of the ecstatic state but also the depths of suffering with which it is bought. Behind the glory of the Transfiguration there will always loom the shadow of the Cross, for " from that time Jesus began to show His disciples how He must go to Jerusalem and suffer many things. . .". Many things, both spiritual and material, cause suffering to the soul in this " Sixth Mansion," for far from investing the contemplative with a kind of Stoic power of endurance, the mystic life enhances and refines his sensibility. There are trials from lack of understanding when the soul is deserted even by her most trusted friends, trials also from failing health, for in this mansion she has almost always to endure severe physical sufferings. But much worse are the spiritual trials, " when there is such aridity that the mind feels as if it had never thought of God nor ever will be able to do so," and when timid directors make her fear that she is a victim of delusions. Mystic prayer itself often becomes a source of the most acute pain, when the separation from the perfect possession of God is felt with an intensity that resembles the pains of Purgatory. Yet the consolations of the soul in this state are such that she makes light of all her sufferings. For ecstasy, the saint says, " is not like a swoon or a fit in which nothing is felt " ; on the contrary, " the soul has never been more alive to spiritual things nor so full of light and of

knowledge of His Majesty as it is now." For while the powers of
the soul are thus suspended, Our Lord discovers to her heavenly
mysteries, and " certain sublime truths are so impressed on the
mind that it needs no other master, for without any effort of its
own Wisdom Himself has enlightened its former ignorance." That
this is so is borne out by the fact that the great ecstatics of the Church
however defective their education, have almost always been of an
extraordinary surety of touch in their doctrine. Whether we
take St. Catherine of Siena, St. Catherine of Genoa, or the humble
Curé d'Ars, their insight into the mysteries of the faith is com-
mensurate only with the sublimity of their ecstatic life, in which
they are taught, like St. Paul, Divine secrets that it is not lawful for
man to utter.

And together with this progressive intellectual illumination
there goes, for St. Teresa as for so many other mystics, an increasing
activity. In her case we have the inestimable advantage that her
mystic graces and her practical achievements can be traced almost
step by step. Her first rapture, which marks the beginning of her
ecstatic state, occurred in 1558 ; her transverberation, together
with her vow of perfection, followed in 1559 ; and two years later,
while her mystic life was steadily growing in fulness, her life of
action began with the difficult foundation of St. Joseph at Avila.
Meant by herself to be a retreat where to satisfy her desire for
prayer and mortification in the years remaining to her, it was
destined by God to be the cradle of the Reform of her Order,
the work in which she literally consumed herself to the last reserves
of her strength. From now on one foundation followed another,
each one of them accompanied by the most extraordinary difficulties—from ecclesiastical superiors threatening excommunication
to hysterical princesses insisting on being accepted as postulants
and recalcitrant landlords going back on their promises. Teresa,
the ecstatic who would fall down in a rapture at the song of a
novice at recreation, bargained with businessmen, talked theology
with bishops, wrote diplomatic letters to the king and governed
her convents with the consummate wisdom of the most experienced
superior-general, so that the Dominican Father Hernandez could
truly say of her : " She is a man, and more of a man than any
man I ever met."

All this is very difficult to understand unless we constantly
remember that all the exterior phenomena of the higher mystic

states are really only accidental, that the one great essential reality is that the mystics live by the Gifts of the Holy Ghost, and especially by the Gift of Wisdom. And this becomes most obvious in the last stage of the contemplative life, when the physical phenomena cease almost entirely, because the body has become accustomed to the Divine visitations. The soul now enters into the stability of the Mystic Marriage, the highest state that can be reached here on earth, before charity, which is the substance of contemplation, is consummated in the Beatific Vision.

The leitmotif of this, the Seventh Mansion, is peace—a peace that neither sufferings nor upheavals can any more disturb. The soul " feels neither aridity nor any interior troubles," as in the preceding mansions, " but a constant tender recollection of Our Lord," for here " He and the soul rejoice in each other alone in profound silence." This is the state of soul when the greatest of the Christian mysteries, the Divine Life of the Holy Trinity, is revealed to her in a very special manner. " By some mysterious manifestation of the truth," says the saint, " the Three Persons of the Most Blessed Trinity . . . communicate themselves to the soul," and from now on she is hardly ever deprived of the conscious experience of their indwelling.

With the cessation of ecstasies the soul has attained to full spiritual maturity and strength ; henceforth she " remains in her centre with her God." This is the final gift bestowed on us " if we empty ourselves of all that belongs to the creature . . . for the love of God," for then " that same Lord will fill us with Himself." The effects of this Transforming Union are even more marvellous than those of the other Mansions, for it produces " a self-forgetfulness so complete that she (the soul) really appears not to exist . . . nor does she wish to be of any account in anything." At the same time her desire for suffering is increased, though it is less violent, and " she feels a great interior joy when persecuted." Perfectly detached from all creatures, there are only two desires left to her : she " wishes to be either always alone or to be occupied in what profits the souls of others."

The Gifts of the Holy Ghost have completed their work ; the tree, pruned and inoculated by the Divine Gardener, brings forth fruit a hundredfold. In the persecutions unleashed by the Mitigated branch of her Order, St. Teresa will stand firm, advising, encouraging, accepting humiliations, for, as she herself says, a soul in this last state of the mystic life " is far more active than before in all that concerns God's service."

But has she not now at last lost her human sensibility in this perfect transformation that divinises the soul, endowing it with a superhuman courage and power of endurance ? Yet sensibility is an integral part of the human being. Again, St. Teresa's own testimony, especially in her letters, shows clearly that here, as everywhere, grace does not destroy but perfect nature. Despite her constant awareness of the indwelling of the Divine Persons in her soul she longs for human understanding, and her letters, especially those to Father Gratian, show the most tender maternal love and care for the well-being of this spiritual son on whom depended so much of the work of the Reform. She also continues to suffer, though very peacefully, from human ingratitude, and nine years after the " Mystic Marriage " she could still write : " How natural it is for us to wish to be recompensed for our love ! "

There is nothing in her of the inhuman reveries about a distorted kind of " disinterested love " which later led the Quietists astray. Through the enjoyment of the fullest and most exalted union with God possible here on earth she became most fully human. Most fully human also in that the typically feminine traits of her character, imaginative powers, strong emotions, sensibility and impulsiveness were brought increasingly under the control of such masculine qualities as capacity for reasoning, self-restraint and orderliness. For the mystics, by living more Divinely, also live more humanly, in the highest sense of the word, having received of the fulness of Him who came that we might have life, and that we might have it more abundantly.

St. Francis de Sales

To ask for nothing, and to refuse nothing.

It is one of the paradoxes of spiritual history that the austere Order of Discalced Carmelites should have been founded by a woman, and the gentle Visitation by a man. The virile St. Teresa wanted her nuns not to be women, but rather " strong men " ; the Bishop of Geneva desired his daughters to be " gentle doves," loving their own insignificance and abjection. It sounds as if these two must be miles apart spiritually—but both, the strength of St. Teresa and the gentleness of St. Francis, were due to grace transforming nature, so that both the virile woman and the tender-hearted man might live the fulness of a human life, in which the limitations even of sex are transcended in a higher unity, where there is neither man nor woman, only a human soul filled with God.

There are many spiritual links between St. Francis de Sales and St. Teresa ; he may almost be said to have discovered the mystic life under the guidance of her writings and of her daughters. Brought up by the Jesuits and remaining for a long time under their direction, his methodical mind fed joyfully on the vigour of the Ignatian Exercises, and well-prepared meditation remained his normal form of prayer until middle life. But in 1604 began his association with Madame de Chantal, to whom the Carmelites of Dijon, fresh from Spain, opened up an entirely new world of contemplative prayer, which the eager Jeanne Françoise soon communicated to her director. But St. Francis was cautious. Those unknown paths might be the right road for those far advanced in the spiritual life—but were they meant for a harassed bishop and a busy woman in the world ? Gradually, however, his resistance gave way, especially as, without seeking for them, he himself experienced mystic states from time to time. His most popular work, the *Introduction to the Devout Life* (1608), contains as yet no mystical teaching properly so called, for the only form of prayer it treats is Meditation. But then it was destined for men and women living in the world, who were beginners in the spiritual life, grappling with the difficulties of the " Purgative way." Hence it must not be inferred from his silence that, at this time, he had not yet experienced mystic prayer himself.

Two years after the first edition of the *Devout Life* he founded the Visitation, together with St. Chantal. Though originally intended for works of mercy and without enclosure, the congregation was soon transformed into a Contemplative Order, and it was for his spiritual daughters that he wrote, in the midst of all the pressure of his episcopal work, his great *Treatise on the Love of God* (finished in 1616) which contains a whole theology of the mystic life.

" To ask for nothing and to refuse nothing "—this was the watchword he gave to the Visitation, as it was the motto of his own life and the very foundation on which he built the edifice of his spiritual teaching. To the superficial reader the words may have almost a ring of Quietism—to ask nothing and to refuse nothing—what then is left to the soul, if she is no longer to have either desires or aversions ? And did not St. Teresa want her daughters to have great desires ?

It is one of the glories of the Church in general and of Catholic mysticism in particular that, for the infinite variety of human characters, there is a rich diversity of means to meet their needs. In Carmel souls are stripped from all attachment to physical comfort, to beauty of sound and colour, to prepare them for the meeting with the Spouse after the Dark Night of the Senses. But the Visitation was designed for those unable to endure the physical hardships of Carmel and the other old Contemplative Orders. Yet self-denial is the sap and food of the spiritual life—so St. Francis transferred it from the senses into the very marrow of the soul, into the Will. For though obedience, of course, curbs self-will in all religious Orders, there is in the Visitation as in St. Francis' *Treatise* a special curbing of the will, even where it is not really self-will. And the form his mystical teaching takes can be fully understood only when his doctrine of " holy indifference " and the death of the will has been grasped.

The Jesuit influence did not cease to act when St. Francis gave up formal meditation for the mystic way—the less so as the Order of St. Ignatius has produced its full quota of mystics, beginning with the founder himself. And so, if St. Ignatius requires his sons to obey " like a corpse," St. Francis desires his daughters to be like statues who, placed in a certain corner by their maker, remain there for no other reason save because he has placed them there, content to be where the sculptor desires them to be, even should he never look at them again. This thought is so dear to him that he develops it in a series of similar comparisons. There is the simile of the wife of St. Louis who, when accompanying her husband on the Crusade, would never ask where he went or what was going to happen next—for she would go wherever her lord chose to take her, content to be near him and to follow where he led. And again there is the comparison of the sick daughter of the physician, who, trusting in the love and wisdom of her father, lets him do with her whatever he chooses without inquiring what treatment he gives her nor why.

It is as if St. Francis could never sufficiently stress the complete

dependence of the soul on her Creator, her perfect indifference
to the means He chooses in regard to her sanctification and, indeed,
to all the circumstances of her interior and exterior life.   This is
the virtue of " holy indifference " which he never tires of extolling.
" The indifferent heart," he says in the *Treatise*," is like a ball of
wax in the hands of God . . . a heart without choice, equally
disposed to all things, without other object of its will save the
will of its God, and whose love is pleased not so much with the
things that God wills, but rather with the will of God that wills
them," for " the good pleasure of God is the sovereign object of
the indifferent soul."   Poor weak humanity almost recoils before
these heights, which even the fiery soul of the austere St. Bernard
considered fully attainable only in the next life.   But St. Francis,
intent only on the most complete surrender of the will to its
God, goes even further and arrives at the impossible demand that
the truly indifferent heart should " rather love hell with the will
of God than heaven without it," and finally, " to imagine the
impossible," as he himself admits, if the indifferent man " knew
that his damnation would be slightly more pleasing to God than
his salvation, he would abandon his salvation and run to his
damnation."

It is at this point that his teaching on indifference would seem
to overreach itself. In the white heat of desire to do the will of
God whatever the cost, such thoughts may perhaps come into a
generous mind.   But, with all the respect due to a Doctor of the
Church, it may be doubted whether such speculations are profitable,
and whether it is not a safer way to exclude from the realm of
" indifference " the petitions of the Pater Noster, which contain,
indeed, the *Fiat voluntas tua*, but also the *Sed libera nos a malo*.

We shall seek in vain for such considerations in a St. Bernard
or St. Catherine, St. Teresa or St. John of the Cross.   Theirs is,
if we may say so, a simple, straightforward, " naïve " mysticism,
running right towards the object of its love without reflecting on
itself and the purity of this love.   Enough for them, to love
God alone and to desire to possess Him alone, for He is " Todo,"
and all else but " Nada "—but as to wondering whether their
love is really pure because it desires the possession of the Beloved,
that lies outside the scope of their contemplation.   For to them
a love that does not desire to possess its object would seem a contradiction in terms.

Yet to St. Francis these speculations are not irrelevant. They are an ingredient of his mystical teaching, giving it a flavour all its own. This taste for subtleties may perhaps be traced to two sources. In the first place, St. Francis de Sales was trained in the school of Duns Scotus and the Jesuits, far more given to hypothetical questionings than the Thomism with which were imbued the masters of St. Catherine and St. John of the Cross. And, secondly, St. Francis is, in a sense, the first of the " modern " mystics—modern taken as implying complications and psychological niceties absent from the medieval and sixteenth century Spanish masters. He says himself in a letter to Madame de Chantal : " No, I certainly am not simple," and he adds : " But strange to say I have a great love for simplicity." It is this almost wistful love of simplicity in a mystic fully conscious of the complexity of his own nature that makes St. Francis de Sales such a sympathetic guide for souls of our own time. And here we touch a second point characteristic of him : even as a mystic he is, above all, the director, visualizing the practical needs of souls. Thus when he deals with mystical prayer he speaks not so much as a mystic analysing his own experiences, nor as a theologian investigating states and phenomena, but pre-eminently as the director giving a practical exposition of the life of prayer for the benefit of his spiritual daughters. It is, however, built on a firm theological foundation, laid in the first five books of the *Treatise*, and interwoven with ardent aspirations which betray that, what he describes, is not alien to his own interior life.

It was, indeed, St. Teresa and the teaching of Carmel which introduced St. Francis to the mystic life ; yet his descriptions and terminology, though dealing with much the same subject matter, are quite different. He frequently follows the earlier masters, especially in his wider use of the term " mystic " and the less rigid classification of the various states of prayer. For far from reserving the word " mystic " for the higher stages of the spiritual life, he affirms that " mental prayer and mystical theology are one and the same thing," and both are " nothing else but a conversation by which the soul communes lovingly with God about His amiable goodness in order to unite herself to it." This " mystical theology " begins with meditation, which is " nothing else but mystic rumination . . . . in order to find motives for love." After a time, when meditation has produced " the honey of devotion . . . . it transforms itself into contemplation," which is " a loving, simple, and permanent attention of the spirit to Divine things," for " meditation is the mother of love, but contemplation is its daughter."

Now what is this contemplation that follows meditation so easily, without any mention of the " night of sense " ? It would seem that it must be equated with what, to-day, is usually called the " Prayer of Simplicity," a simple loving attention to God meant to " alienate us not from the spiritual sense, but from the corporeal senses "—and so precisely what St. John of the Cross calls the " Night of the Senses," though the Carmelite describes it far more dramatically and profoundly as he, called to a more purely contemplative life than the Bishop of Geneva, would have experienced it in a different and more searching way. It holds the same place in St. Francis' mystical ascent as in that of St. John, for it is meant to make us " like angels " and to prepare us for a higher state. This he calls " loving recollection " *recueillement amoureux*, which corresponds to St. Teresa's " Prayer of Quiet," the first stage on the way of passive prayer. For to produce this recollection, he tells his daughters, is not in our power, " but God produces it in us when He so pleases by His holy grace," so that the soul feels His Presence " by the attraction which He produces in the centre of the heart." In this prayer the whole soul is at rest, except the " point of the will which she moves gently and almost imperceptibly."

This *fine pointe de la volonté* is a conception especially dear to the Saint, who uses it again and again to describe the higher operations of the soul. There seems to be every justification for equating it with what medieval speculative mysticism calls *scintilla animæ* or " Ground of the soul " which, in its turn, is closely connected with the *Imago*, that quality of the soul by which she is *capax Dei*, capable of God. This " point of the will," which he also calls the " fine point of the spirit," is the proper seat of the mystical life ; and it can never be sufficiently stressed that this region of the soul, where contemplation takes place, is wholly above the emotions. Only in times of " consolation " will the spirit's unfelt delight in God overflow into these and sometimes even into the senses, so that the mystical Divine Presence in the highest part of the soul can be felt by the whole man. If, however, the Presence is not felt, it does not mean that it is not there—else the mystic life would

no longer be such in times of " aridity " and " desolation "—
states inevitably bound up with it and the most efficacious means
of purification.

It is at these times of dryness that the soul must resemble the
statue which, though it sees not its master, receives a certain
satisfaction from the mere fact that it is where he wants it to be.
Nor, and here speaks the director, must the soul give in to the
temptation, which will arise again and again especially in complicated and introspective natures, to scrutinise her own state ; for
" there is a great difference between being occupied with God
who gives us contentment, and being occupied with the contentment which He gives us." According to the degree of absorption
that this prayer brings the satisfaction will be stronger or less so.
For there are several degrees in this prayer : sometimes all the
faculties of the soul will be occupied by it, at other times only the
will. In the higher stages he speaks of " liquefaction," and the
whole description differs considerably from St. Teresa, in that
the physical effects are less clear and the terminology is vaguer,
as in the case of " ecstasy," which seems here to be used in a much
wider sense. This is how he describes " liquefaction " : " An
extreme complacency of the lover in the Beloved produces a
certain spiritual impotence which renders the soul incapable of
remaining within herself. Therefore . . . . she lets herself go
out and flow into what she loves. This she does not by an upward
jerk, nor does she press (herself to the Beloved) as in union, but
she goes gently, flowing like a liquid into the Divinity she loves
. . . . This flowing of the soul into God is a veritable ecstasy
by which the soul is all outside her natural being, all absorbed
into God." The soul, thus drawn into God, yet cannot love Him
as fully as she would wish, and this unfulfilled desire produces
in her the " Wound of Love." St. Teresa, too, speaks of the wound
of love ; but there seems here, as in the meaning of ecstasy and later
in the description of rapture, a subtle difference between the conceptions of St. Francis and those of the Carmelite. For in St.
Teresa's account the " Wound of Love'' is brought about by a
real mystic happening which takes place only in the fully developed
ecstatic state, when the soul is actually wounded in a mysterious
manner. In St. Francis' description, on the other hand, the whole
is pre-eminently a psychological event, the " wound " being an
almost metaphorical expression of the subjective feeling of frus-

tration in the soul who desires to love God more than she is actually capable of doing.

The higher we ascend in what is called the " passive " states of prayer, the more marked become the differences in the mystic theology of the two Saints.   There is an unmistakable dissimilarity of spiritual atmosphere in their descriptions of union and ecstasy (in the narrower sense) which is quite striking, though at first difficult to account for.   But, looking closely at the two concep- tions of the " Wound of Love " and at the Salesian definition of ecstasy as a ravishment by which " we go out and remain out of and above ourselves in order to unite ourselves to God " we may perhaps arrive at a plausible explanation.   The clue seems to lie in the words " in order to unite ourselves to God " (*pour nous unir a Dieu*).   They express clearly a self-determined activity of the soul even in ecstasy, though, as goes without saying, under the strong influence of Divine grace.   That this is not an isolated instance is proved by the description that follows :   admiration of the understanding, produced by the things shown to us by God, " takes us out of and above ourselves, and by the vivid attention and application of our understanding to heavenly things, it throws us into ecstasy."   In like manner the will elevates itself to God and " leaving all its earthly inclinations it enters into ravishment." It is always the human factor, the admiring understanding or the loving will, that has its own active part to play even in the " passive " states *par excellence* by " applying " or " elevating " itself.   St. Francis de Sales describes the same states of soul as St. Teresa ; but the emphasis is different.   In his presentation of the mystic life the part of the soul is in the fore-front of the picture, whilst in the last " mansions " of the *Interior Castle* God is the sole actor.

It seems a paradox that precisely the Saint who insists so strongly on " annihilation " and complete " indifference " on the ascetical side of the spiritual life should give so much to the human activity when it comes to mystical prayer.   Is it too fanciful to see in this combination, too, the influence of his Jesuit training ?   The mystic life is the fullest flowering of the life of grace, and it is in their doctrine of grace that the Jesuit school of theology attributes more to human effort than the Thomists.   This difference of emphasis in the theological foundations necessarily shows itself in the spiritual doctrine and the interpretation of the mystic life and probably even in the colouring, if the metaphor be permitted of the mystical experiences themselves. St. Teresa, though deeply indebted to the Jesuits for the ascetical side of her development, received her doctrinal education mainly from the Dominicans— a tradition which remained alive in her Order : the theology of St. John of the Cross is Thomist, and the later Carmelite school of Salamanca even more so. It is the Dominican emphasis on the Divine action that penetrates, though not consciously, Teresan spirituality ; it is the Jesuit stress on the human co-operation that gives the Salesian doctrine its peculiarly " modern " flavour.

Of the twelve books of the *Treatise of the Love of God* only two, the sixth and the seventh, deal with prayer. The other ten surrounding them treat of the Love of God in its bearing on the whole Christian life, apart from prayer, and most of all on the transformation it works in the will and in the life of the virtues. These books are a treasure house of practical spiritual wisdom and a perfect guide to that most precious possession of Christians, the peace that surpasses all understanding. There are few mystics who have been more insistent preachers of peace and tranquillity than St. Francis de Sales. Director as he was of a host of excitable French ladies, he knew how inimical to the spiritual life is commotion and upheavals. How many of his penitents may not have come to him with their " inspirations," believed to be from above, demanding to be immediately released from their boring everyday duties in order to follow a higher vocation. Perhaps it is with their claims in view that he gives this luminous description of the surest sign of genuine inspiration : " Perseverance against inconstancy and levity, peace and gentleness of heart as opposed to restlessness and worries, humble obedience as against self-will and extravagance." And this gentleness of heart on which he insists so much is best learned in afflictions, where true love is both tested and deepened.

St. Francis de Sales is sometimes called " the gentle Saint." Yet his gentleness is somewhat deceptive, for it goes together with an extraordinary austerity. But this austerity is all, as it were, interior—an austerity of the will rather than of the senses. What is particularly misleading about him is his style, the abundance of imagery, of milk and honey, flowers and bees and little birds with which his books are teeming. But underneath all this sweetness there is a rock. And the rock is revealed in his attitude to suffering, where he is every whit as exacting as St. John of the Cross

I

himself. Voluntary penances, fasts, vigils and the like are indeed good, but better than all this and far more pleasing to God will it be " when we receive with patience, gently and sweetly the pains, torments and tribulations (sent to us by God), considering the Divine will that sends them to us. But then is love truly excellent, when we receive the afflictions not only gently and patiently, but when we cherish, love and caress them, because of the Divine good pleasure from which they proceed. Now, among all the pursuits of perfect love, that which is done by the spirit's acquiescence in spiritual tribulations is without doubt the most refined and elevated achievement."

So the gentle St. Francis, too, has known the " Dark Night of the Spirit "—and to him, too, it is the touchstone of true spirituality. It may almost be said to be the decisive characteristic of heterodox devotion that it aims at a " mysticism without tears." Whether we take Molinos or Madame Guyon, or any of the so-called " nature mystics," they all endeavour to find a " mystic " way that will smoothly carry them past the Cross. But the Cross is precisely at the centre of the mystic life, and there is no surer and shorter way to mystic union than through it. One cannot be had without the other, that is the burden of all mystic teaching and experience, because Christianity without the Cross is a contradiction in terms, and mysticism is Christianity in its highest and purest form.

" To ask for nothing and to refuse nothing "—though the demand may sound easy and even trivial, it is a principle that, understood as St. Francis understands it, involves a degree of self-stripping possible only in the higher walks of sanctity. It is his great glory that he has taught this way to the summits of Mount Carmel to those who, because of their physical weakness, thought themselves incapable of reaching it. And so the Order, which he founded, was destined to become the birthplace of the modern devotion to the Sacred Heart, the great Lover of those who, however infirm and heavy-laden, are yet fully capable of learning from Him, because nothing more is required than to be " meek and humble of heart "—but only those who have tried to fulfil the demand know the cost.

CHAPTER VI

Todo Y Nada : St. John of the Cross

At eventide, they will examine thee on Love.—St. John of the Cross.

St. John of the Cross has been called "The mystics' mystic." He is the mystic Doctor of the Church, in him both mystic doctrine and mystic experience are united in a perfect unity. The very titles of his works contain an outline of the mystic life : the first task is the Ascent of Mount Carmel, the painful climb often in the aridity of the senses and the Dark Night of the Soul. But this is only the way : at its end the soul, filled with joy, will sing her Spiritual Cànticle, ultimately to find herself transformed into a Living Flame of Love.

St. John of the Cross is a lover, and only as a lover can he be understood. All his terrifying self-abnegation that frightens the beginner, his penances, his thirst for sufferings and humiliations, all this is but the expression of a soul on fire with love. The children of this world are so often wiser than the children of the light—when they desire something they spend their whole energy, their whole strength to obtain it. The man in love with a woman uses all his resources, all manner of strategems to win her ; the ambitious man leaves nothing undone, no " avenue " unexplored, to " get on " in life, the lover of money thinks night and day of shares and dividends—but how few who call themselves Christians are really spending their whole substance in Christ's service ? St. John of the Cross was such a one. His whole life was one great race towards the goal, run with ever-increasing speed and without a moment's slackening.

He was not, like St. Bernard, a counsellor of Popes and kings. He was not, like St. Francis de Sales, the founder of a new Order, and his activities in the reform of Carmel were secondary to the work of St. Teresa. His vocation was to be a mystic, *the* mystic *par excellence.* Now that word comes from the Greek myein, that is to close one's lips or eyes, and so to be hidden. For the mystic life is a hidden life, it seeks not the limelight. It hides itself like the leaven is hidden in the lump of dough. Like the leaven it works in secret, unperceived, and like the leaven, it transforms the whole lump. So the mystic life of St. John of the Cross was lived in perfect obscurity. The young religious at Duruelo, that smallest and poorest of Spanish convents, the confessor of a nuns' monastery at Avila, the captive in the dark dungeon at Toledo, the prior of the Carmelite convent at Granada, and, lastly, the maltreated dying little friar at Ubeda—where is there a Doctor of the Church more hidden than he? His life was truly hidden with Christ in God.

Vos estis sal terræ the Church reads in her Office on the feast of a Doctor. Salt is hidden, is inconspicuous, but it both seasons and preserves the food which without it would be tasteless and rot. The works of St. John of the Cross have sustained innumerable souls and preserved them from illusion and despair. The *Ascent of Mount Carmel* is a real ascent, a hard, arduous climb, and he who has attempted to read it through in the first fervour of his spiritual life knows how often he has been compelled to stop for breath, yes, and even to lay it aside with a sigh : This is too hard, surely it cannot be meant for me. And then, perhaps, he has opened his New Testament : " If any man would come after me, let him deny himself and take up his cross. . . ." " If any man comes unto me and hates not his father, mother. . . . yea and his own life also, he cannot be my disciple. . . ." " No man can serve two masters. . . ." And, maybe, he realizes that the *Ascent of Mount Carmel* is but a commentary on the teaching of Our Lord, and he will take courage and continue the climb up to the summit of Mount Carmel, which stands for both, Mount Thabor and Mount Calvary, because in this life one cannot be had without the other.

From the beginning the Saint makes it perfectly clear that his teaching on abnegation is but a means to an end, not an end in itself. The very first words of the Prologue to the *Ascent* speak of " this dark night, through which the soul passes, in order to attain to the Divine light of the perfect union of the love of God." It is a thoroughfare, a tunnel, as it were, through which the soul must needs pass, but which is to be desired only because it will lead to the goal, " the perfect union of the love of God, as far as is possible in this life " ; and while man is painfully making his way through the terrors of the " Dark Night," he endures them gladly in the certitude that they will lead him into the glorious light of day, which the eyes of his soul could not endure unless they had been made strong in this " Dark Night." This sounds like a paradox, but it is not a paradox. For what seems to the soul like a "Night" is in reality only the blinding force of the Divine Light, which on the insufficiently purified beginner has the effect of darkness, because he is not yet strong enough to endure it. This darkness and aridity can cause the most intense suffering to the soul, especially if she does not know what is happening to her. Therefore St. John of the Cross, moved by the charity of the contemplative who desires for his brethren the goal he himself has already reached, undertakes to guide them to this summit.

It is often said that St. John of the Cross is dangerous reading, that he is apt to unsettle souls and make them lose their balance. In answer to this two points may be made. First, the Carmelite mystic is a Doctor of the Church, and it does not seem likely that the Mother of us all should propose to us a Master who will lead us astray. But, secondly, every good thing may become harmful if it be used in the wrong way. A warming fire, if not guarded, may cause a conflagration, a knife to cut our food may become an instrument for killing, yes, and even a soft cushion in Othello's hands may murder a young wife. St. John of the Cross says at the end of his Prologue : " Nor is my principal intent to address all, but rather certain persons of our sacred Order of Mount Carmel . . . . who, as they are already detached from the temporal things of this world, will better understand the instruction concerning detachment of spirit." The important words of this restrictive passage are not the " certain persons of our sacred Order of Mount Carmel "—the *Ascent* is a book not only for Carmelites, but for all those who would reach union with God, else St. John of the Cross would not have been proclaimed Doctor of the Universal Church. The important words are " who . . . . are already detached from the temporal things of this world."

And here another point needs clearing up. The *Ascent* is sometimes called a book for beginners. This is true, provided the term be given the right definition. If we mean by beginners men and women newly converted from the world, who still struggle against temptation to mortal sin in the " Purgative Way," who meditate with difficulty for about a quarter of an hour and who find it hard to give up their morning sleep to go to Mass—if we thus understand the term, then the *Ascent of Mount Carmel* is decidedly *not* meant for beginners. On the contrary, the attempt of such persons to follow its rigorous teaching would lead only to confusion, and possibly, even to spiritual disaster. Yet the *Ascent* is a book for beginners, for beginners, that is, in the mystic life, of which it describes the initial stages. These " beginners " have already left the attractions of this world behind, whether they are in the cloister or trying to lead mortified lives in the world. God has already drawn them from the blandishments of sense and from worldly ambition by making them taste and see that the Lord is sweet. They have, for some time, enjoyed the sensible consolations of a fervent life, and, very naturally, have become attached to their spiritual joys. These are the " beginners " for whom the *Ascent* is written, souls who probably consider themselves, and are considered by others, strong in virtue and shining examples for their weaker brethren. The *Ascent* is meant to destroy these fond illusions which, if persisted in, will make progress in the spiritual life impossible.

The means that brings these souls to the knowledge of their faults is the " Night of the Senses," " occurring," as the Saint says, " at the time when God begins to bring them into the state of contemplation "—a further description that leaves no doubt as to whom he means by " beginners." This Night begins with the perfect mortification of all the desires of the soul, even such apparently legitimate ones as desire for created beauty, for knowledge, for prelacy. For, says the Saint, " All the wealth and glory of all the creatures, in comparison with the wealth which is God, is supreme poverty and wretchedness."

It is important to grasp what he means by such language, which may easily be misunderstood. St. John of the Cross is no Manichean, he does not hold creatures to be evil in themselves. But he is so enamoured of the absolute perfection of God and so conscious of the fatal attraction which the imperfect beauty of the world exercises on fallen human nature that he uses the strongest language to dissuade souls from letting themselves be ensnared by it. For, he says, " any desire, although it be for but the smallest imperfection, stains and defiles the soul," and he quotes Our Lord's words reported by St. Luke : " He that renounces not all things that he possesses cannot be my disciple." This teaching, however, as he explicitly states, does not apply to those natural desires which " are not consented to nor pass beyond the first movements (that is, all those wherein the rational will has no part, whether at first or afterward) ; and to take away these—that is, to mortify them wholly in this life—is impossible. And these hinder not the soul in such a way as to prevent attainment to Divine Union, even though they be not, as I say, wholly mortified ; for the natural man may well have them, and yet the soul may be quite free from them according to the rational spirit." With this restriction, then, must be understood the hard saying : " It is supreme ignorance for the soul to think that it will be able to pass to this high estate of union with God if first it void not the desire of all things, natural and supernatural, which may hinder it."

Which are these desires for natural things that may hinder the soul's progress ? They are not so much passing desires for this or that, but habitual attachments—and the list he gives of them may well strike terror into many hearts : " These habitual imperfections are, for example, a common custom of much speaking, or some attachment which we never wish entirely to conquer—such as that to a person, a garment, a book, a cell, a particular kind of food. . . . While it (the soul) has this there is no possibility that it will make progress in perfection, even though the imperfection may be extremely small. For it is the same thing if a bird be held by a slender cord or by a stout one ; since, even if it be slender, the bird will be as well held as though it were stout, for so long as it breaks it not and flies not away." And, as if this were not enough, a few pages later we read these awe-inspiring counsels : " strive always to choose, not that which is easiest, but that which is most difficult ; not that which is most delectable, but that which is most unpleasing ; not that which gives most pleasure, but rather that which gives least ; not that which is restful, but that which is wearisome ; not that which gives consolation, but rather that which makes disconsolate. . . . "

Would not such passages as these seem to justify Huysman's picture of the gloomy ascetic " terrible, sanglant et les yeux secs " ? And then we remember how, in the days of Duruelo, he let come his mother and brother and sister-in-law to keep house for the brethren, we remember how, later on, he wrote mournfully about his sojourn among the Andalusians whom he disliked, yearning to return to Castile ; we think of the lovely story of the asparagus he desired to eat on his last journey shortly before his death—and we ask ourselves : did he, then, not practise himself what he taught ?

There are similar apparent inconsistencies in the lives of other mystics. There is St. Bernard of the terrifying austerities, weeping like a child over his dead brother. There is St. Catherine, warning her niece, who is a young nun, in the strongest terms against any but the most strictly professional relations with her confessors, while she herself is surrounded by her spiritual family of clergy and laymen. There is St. Teresa, keeping her nuns in complete seclusion, while she herself cries for a little comfort from Father Gratian. Are all these canonised Saints following the Pharisaic device : Do according to my words, but not according to my deeds ?

There is another side to the matter. Before St. Catherine associated freely with her "spiritual family" she had been living for years in the strictest retirement without speaking to anyone except her family without leave from her confessor. When St. Teresa found consolation in the friendship with Gratian she was nearing her end, having long been in full enjoyment of the Transforming Union. And before St. John of the Cross thought of calling his family to Duruelo he had for years been practising his teaching on detachment with the utmost rigour. "Perfect love casteth out fear," or, as St. Augustine has it : "Love and do what thou wilt." But this love is permitted to do as it wills precisely because it is perfectly purified and therefore has no other will but the will of God. This gives us the clue both to the terrifying maxims of St. John of the Cross and the seeming inconsistency in some traits of his own life. We can see his stern teaching in its right perspective only if we keep our eyes steadfastly on the end to which it is meant to lead. The green moist wood of human attachments and desires is so ruthlessly dried up by penance and abnegation only that it may one day be consumed in the living flame of love. This is the goal, the incorruptible crown of which St. Paul speaks, to obtain which we must bruise our body and bring it into subjection. And not our body only, but also our soul which, according to St. John of the Cross, we must void of all things, natural and supernatural, which may hinder it.

Natural and supernatural—this sounds strange indeed. Are there, then, even in the realm of the supernatural things that may prevent our union with God ? Can such *gratiæ gratis datæ* as sweet feelings of devotion, visions, locutions, etc. be obstacles rather than helps in the spiritual progress ?

Here we must distinguish. These graces, like all God's gifts, are meant to benefit us—but their efficacy depends in large measure on the use we make of them. They are valuable means to an end if they are treated as such ; that is, if they are not desired for their own sake and for the pleasure they give us, they will further our sanctification. But human nature is always tempted to covet the things that give it satisfaction because of this satisfaction, and so will prize the gifts rather than the Giver, to whom they are intended to lead. When this danger becomes acute—and it is the common experience that this is an almost inevitable development—the soul is brought into a state which St. John of the Cross calls the Dark Night. This Night, as the Saint points out, has an active and a passive part ; that is, normally, there will be an interaction between God and the soul. On the one hand, the soul will further God's designs by voiding herself of all that is repugnant to the Divine Union ; on the other, God Himself will produce in her a spiritual emptiness in order to detach her completely from all that is not He. This spiritual Night is brought about by the three theological virtues which empty the three faculties of the soul : faith is a darkness to the understanding which cannot comprehend what is proposed to it ; hope is a night to the memory, voiding it of its contents, and charity empties the will of all earthly affections, drawing it entirely to God. These three "Nights" are absolutely essential for spiritual progress, and the Saint has very hard words for those who "think that it suffices to deny themselves worldly things without annihilating and purifying themselves of spiritual attachment."

"Wherefore," he says, "it comes to pass that, when there presents itself to them any of this solid and perfect spirituality, consisting in the annihilation of all sweetness in God, in aridity, distaste and trial, which is the true spiritual cross, and the detachment of the spiritual poverty of Christ, they flee from it as from death, and seek only sweetness and delectable communion with God. This is not self-denial and detachment of spirit, but spiritual gluttony." For the true lover of Christ will seek Him on the Cross rather than on Mount Thabor, and the words of St. John are no more severe than Our Lord's rebuke to St. Peter when he presumed to hold Him back on the way that was to lead to Golgotha : Get thee behind me, Satan. . . .

The soul, then, that would reach the mystic goal, must take

courage and renounce all consolation. This, however, is not to say that she must refuse the consolation that is offered—that will often not be possible, even if it were desirable—but she must prepare herself to forgo it willingly if it be withdrawn. This practice of detachment is the active part of the Night, and once a man has trained himself in it and is resolved to bear whatever crosses it may please the Lord to send him, " he will find in them all great relief and sweetness." For we may be pardoned for insisting that the ascetic teaching of St. John of the Cross however severe and forbidding it may sound, is meant only to lead to union, and in this union even the bitterest Cross becomes sweet, because it is borne for love ; and the Divine Love Who said : My yoke is sweet and My burden is light, will Himself ease its weight.

The reason for the necessity of all this painful practice of detachment is that union with God is not achieved through the understanding and still less through feelings or the imagination, but only through " faith, which alone is the proximate and proportionate means whereby the soul is united with God." And then St. John, the director and theologian, launches out into a detailed description of all the obstacles the soul may encounter on her road in the darkness of faith, and of the manner in which she must face them, so that they may cause her " not harm, but profit." He begins with external apparitions, auditions, sweet smells, savours and touches, which, he says," are wont to come to spiritual persons." We must remember that St. John of the Cross wrote in sixteenth–century Spain, and that he drew his experiences largely from unlettered, highly-strung nuns, from nuns, moreover, who were denied almost all the satisfactions that music, literature and art give to the senses and the emotions, and who would, therefore, be the more inclined to satisfy the cravings of their nature by a spiritual life supplying for these deficiencies. Their Carmelite director utters the gravest warnings against these exciting experiences, which " very easily become the means whereby error and presumption grow in the soul ; since, as they are so palpable and material, they stir the senses greatly. . . . Thus the soul goes after them, abandoning faith." For faith is dark and quite beyond the realm of the senses, therefore, " the more attention it (the soul) pays to such things, the farther it strays from the true way. . . ." Moreover, the devil may have a part in all these things that delight the senses, " these representations and feelings,

both the spiritual and the sensual part of the soul " since," says the Saint, " the one is never truly purged without the other," for " all the imperfections and disorders of the sensual part have their strength and root in the spirit." This Night is caused by the excess of the Divine Light now streaming into the soul, which darkens her natural intelligence and causes her pain. This pain arises from the presence of opposites in the soul, whose imperfections struggle against the Divine Perfections. For " when this pure light assails the soul, in order to expel its impurity, the soul feels itself to be so impure and miserable that it believes God to be against it," an experience described by many Saints. This conviction that God has forsaken her is one of the most searching trials possible in this life, the supreme dereliction of Our Lord on the Cross, which St. John seems to have experienced in the prison at Toledo. This feeling of being utterly abandoned, of being cast off from the friendship of God, is not to be compared with the Night of Sense. This means aridity, but the Night of the Spirit spells desolation. In this desolation God, as it were, " assails " the soul—at least so she feels His action, which in itself is light and gentle, but to her impurity becomes heavy and oppressive. Nor is this the only pain she has to suffer in this state. For the soul " feels, too, that all creatures have forsaken it, and that it is condemned by them, particularly by its friends." We are at once reminded of St. Catherine, overwhelmed with detractions from her fellow-tertiaries ; of St. Teresa, regarded by her confessor as a restless woman deluded by the devil ; of St. Margaret Mary, persecuted by her superiors for her revelations. For the lives of the mystics are particularly faithful reproductions of the life of Our Lord : as He was betrayed by Judas, abandoned by His disciples in the supreme hour of need, and denied even by St. Peter, the rock on which His Church was to be built, so they have to suffer in their affections even from those most closely related to them by spiritual ties. " Thus in herself this afflicted soul can find no good, being conscious only of the deepest poverty and wretchedness," and from others she receives only reproaches and contradiction. " For the sensual part," says St. John, " is purified in aridity, the faculties are purified in the emptiness of their apprehensions, and the spirit is purified in thick darkness."

And even should the soul in this state find a director who understands her, " its director's advice," writes St. John, " contains no remedy for its troubles . . . . for until the Lord shall have completely purged it after the manner that He wills, no means or remedy is of any service or profit for the relief of its afflictions," one of the most painful of which is her all but complete inability to pray. "In truth," says the Saint, "this is no time for the soul to speak with God; it should rather put its mouth in the dust, as Jeremiah says, so that perchance there may come to it some present hope, and it may endure its purgation with patience." Nor is there any chance for the soul of distracting herself from this state of suffering, as she can pay no attention to anything that may occupy her, for this dark contemplation absorbs her completely. For this "Divine ray of contemplation," which assails the soul with its Divine light, "transcends the natural power of the soul, and herein it darkens it and deprives it of all natural affections and apprehensions . . . .; and thus it leaves it not only dark, but likewise empty, according to its faculties and desires, both spiritual and natural. And, by thus leaving it empty and in darkness, it purges and illuminates it with Divine spiritual light even when the soul thinks not that it has this light, but believes itself to be in darkness." But, though this light is seemingly darkness, it illuminates the soul with wonderful power, giving her a wisdom, penetration, and discernment of spiritual things far superior to what she had before this "Night" assailed her; for now the spirit is being purged in regard to all particular affections and objects of the understanding and taught to see all things in God as far as is possible in this world. For the object of all these painful purgations, which must be constantly kept in view in order to understand the saint as he wishes to be understood, is perfect union with God. For this Night brings darkness to the spirit "only to give it light in everything," "although it humbles it and makes it miserable, it does so only to exalt it and raise it up; and, although it impoverishes it and empties it of all natural affection and attachment, it does so only that it may enable it to stretch forward, divinely, and thus to have fruition and experience of all things, both above and below, yet to preserve its unrestricted liberty of spirit in them all."

This, then, is the goal: the "Spiritual Betrothal," and, later, the "Spiritual Marriage" or the Transforming Union, by which the soul is brought, after passing through the valley of darkness, into the Divine liberty of the children of God. When the Cruci-

fixion is completed, and the soul, in the most intimate union with
Our Lord, has made her ultimate surrender, "into thy Hands
I commend my spirit," the Resurrection is not far distant, Good
Friday is followed by Easter, the humiliation of Calvary by the
glory of the Risen Lord. The "Dark Night of the Soul" is
passed, and, freed from her imperfections, she joyously begins
to sing her "Spiritual Canticle."

The book that bears this title is a Commentary of his wonderful
poem, the first part of which was composed by the Saint in the
prison of Toledo, describing the gradual emergence of the soul
from the last shades of the Night into the glorious dawn of morning.
The *Canticle* opens with the sighs of the loving soul for her Beloved,
who, after giving her "sweet and delectable communion with
Him," has left her "dry and alone" ; in a dryness, however, that
is "wholly cauterised with the fire of love" and already instinct
with the expectation of a speedy healing of the "wound of love"
which she has received. Thus the reminiscence of the Dark
Night described in the previous work is still there—indeed it is as
little absent from the highest stages of the mystic life as is the
memory of the Cross from the joys of Easter, but, like the Death
of Calvary, it is now transfigured by the light of day. For the
sufferings of the soul at this stage proceed no longer from aridity
and desolation, but rather from "enkindling touches of love,"
which leave her aflame with ardent desire and the painful though
"delectable" longing to die in order to be fully united to her
Beloved : "For there is shown to them in glimpses an immense
good and it is not granted to them ; wherefore their affliction and
torment are unspeakable."

For the loving soul can be satisfied by none but God Himself,
and in her longing cries out "Surrender Thou Thyself now completely" and complains : "Since Thou hast wounded this heart,
wherefore didst thou not heal it ? " For the more deeply the soul
is wounded by love, the more impatient she becomes, "because,
having wounded her heart, He did not heal it by slaying it wholly"
but leaves her in the state of a sick man, sighing for health. For
"the loving soul cannot fail to desire the recompense and wages
of its love, for the sake of which recompense it serves the Beloved,
for otherwise its love would not be true ; the which wages and
recompense are naught else . . . . than greater love, until it
attains to being in perfection of love . . . . in order to find

K

complete refreshment there . . . . which is the perfection and fulfilment of loving God."

Here we are at the core and centre of St. John's teaching on perfect abnegation and its *raison d'être*, which is perfect love. What is perhaps most striking is, that the author of the *Dark Night*, unlike St. Francis de Sales, frankly admits that the soul thirsts for full union with God in perfect love. The thought seems never to have entered his mind that "disinterested" love might be carried so far that the soul should wish to be separated from God even eternally, should this be His will. His whole life, his very being, is burning with desire fror the complete possession of his only love. Nada, yes, but only to attain to Todo. "In order to arrive at possessing everything, desire to possess nothing." Is St. John of the Cross, then, perhaps less unselfish in his love than the Founder of the Visitation ? The very formulation of this question reveals its absurdity. But St. John is a very different character. St. Francis de Sales was subtle by temperament and training ; his mystic life was wisely restrained and penetrated by a self-scrutiny intent on detecting flaws even in the desire for eternal beatitude. St. John of the Cross is not subtle. It never occurred to him to question the purity of his love as long as it desired the possession of God alone. The modern temptation to equate the God-given desire for happiness with selfishness was far from his soul, wholly intent on being united to the one Being whose possession is Beatitude. He saw clearly that love would not be love if it did not desire to possess what it loves as fully as possible, and unblushingly his soul entreats the Lord to quench her desires with His Presence, for "naught else suffices but the possession of the Beloved."

The mystic life, as we have insisted before, is the life of love *par excellence*, of which all earthly loves are but dim shadows. For earthly love is limited by its object, which is finite, and always subject to God, above Whom or even equally with Whom, no creature can be loved without sin. But man's love for God has an infinite object, and it is not only permitted, but commanded to absorb the whole of man, taking precedence over all other, however legitimate, affections. Therefore, once a man resolves to devote his whole being to the love of God, he will be instructed in the science of love in a way far surpassing any earthly conception, and the only obstacle he encounters on his road will be his own incapacity to love as much as he desires and as he knows the object of his love to deserve it.

The whole being of St. John of the Cross is penetrated by this love which yearns for fulfilment. For true love is "ecstatic," that is, it goes out of itself towards the Beloved, never stopping to reflect whether it might, perhaps, be more perfect not to desire fulfilment. For it knows that the Spouse desires His bride even more ardently than she desires Him, so why should she fear to displease Him by her impetuous longing ? And so in the dark dungeon of Toledo the enraptured friar sings boldly his love, " for in those that are in love with each other the wound of one is the wound of both," and " in the lover, love is a flame which burns with the desire of burning more." Only when the soul is introduced into the happy state which he calls " Spiritual Betrothal " does she begin to enter " into an estate of peace and delight and sweetness of love " which he hymns as " the silent music, the sounding solitude, the supper that recreates and enkindles love." Here the soul finds the food that truly satisfies her, she receives high wisdom and tastes wondrous delights, and the heart of the lover, the poet and the mystic overflows in an ecstasy of words that communicate even to those who have never been near these heights a shadow of those things that God gives to His darlings.

In this state He gives to the soul a knowledge of Himself which is " most lofty and most delectable," touching her very substance and overflowing into the understanding. The whole human being is satisfied in this communication of " purely spiritual visions or revelations," infinitely superior to those received in the Illuminative Way, though the soul always remains in the obscurity of faith, in which she receives in God " a dark and profound Divine intelligence." But this " tranquil night," as the Saint calls it, " is not as the dark night, but as the night which is already near the rising of the morning : for this calm and quiet in God is not complete darkness to the soul, as is the dark night, but it is tranquillity and quiet in the Divine light, in a new knowledge of God, wherein the spirit is most gently tranquil, being raised to the Divine light." All the painful purgations, all the emptyings of the human spirit, are now seen to be but ways to the glorious goal ; for " in this tranquillity the understanding sees itself raised up in a new and strange way, above all natural understanding, to the Divine light."

For the mystic union produces not a Quietist dulling of the understanding, but its supernatural illumination, and the transitory emptiness of the Dark Night is only a prelude to the new fulness : *In lumine tuo videbimus lumen.*   Souls so enlightened and filled with the sweetness that God gives them " run very quickly upon the way of perfection," for now it is not so much themselves that run, but God who draws them : *Trahe me, post te curremus in odorem unguentorum tuorum.*   Thus they are at last introduced into the " inner cellar," which " is the last and most intimate degree of love to which the soul may attain in this life," and for this, says the Saint, " it will be needful that the Holy Spirit shall take my hand and move my pen."

Here we approach the Transforming Union, the forecourts of heaven, as it were, in which the Gifts of the Holy Ghost attain complete dominion over the soul.   Here in the " inner cellar " the soul is allowed to drink freely of her Beloved.   " For according to the understanding it drinks wisdom and knowledge ; according to the will it drinks sweetest love ; and according to the memory, it drinks recreation and delight in the remembrance and sense of glory," and so all the three faculties of the soul are satisfied together. In comparison with the light she now receives " the knowledge of the whole world is pure ignorance "—an experience which made a St. Thomas exclaim that all he had written was but straw. " For now my exercise is in loving alone," says St. John of the Cross ; all his doing and suffering is nothing but the " exercise of love," the sole occupation of the Bride-Soul, whose virtues are a garland of perfections, bound by the thread of charity, the *vinculum perfectionis.*   All this beauty of the soul is the work of grace, which makes her worthy to be loved by God.   " For (she says) if thou didst find me swarthy, now canst thou indeed look upon me, since thou didst look upon me and leave in me grace and beauty." Now the Holy Ghost breathes through the soul to prepare her for the visit of the Son of God, who will transform her entirely into Himself, in the highest state, the Spiritual Marriage, which the Saint holds to be " never without confirmation in grace."   " For," he says, " even as in the consummation of marriage according to the flesh the two become one flesh . . . even so, when this Spiritual Marriage between God and the soul is consummated, there are two natures in one spirit and love of God."

Words must necessarily fail to describe this state, " wherein is effected such union of the two natures and such communication of the Divine nature to the human, that, while neither of them changes its being, each of them appears to be God . . . it surpasses everything that can be described," for the soul is now strong with the strength of God, " with its neck reclining on the gentle arms of the Beloved," and neither the devil nor the world nor the flesh is able to molest her any more. In this state she learns the highest of the Divine secrets, " for true and perfect love can keep nothing hidden," particularly the mysteries of the Incarnation and Redemption. All fears have ceased, she is hardly able even to feel compassion and sorrow any more ; for she is now almost like the angels, performing the works of mercy, but without such human feelings as pity and grief. Instead she is always filled with rejoicing, for there is a spring in her, " the water whereof, as Christ says through St. John, springs up to eternal life," and all the sensual part is fully surrendered to the spirit. For now at last the soul has regained her original purity :

> The little white dove has returned to the ark with the bough,
> And now the turtle-dove has found the mate of her desire
> on the green banks.

This, however, does not mean that the soul is now incapable of suffering. On the contrary, she desires it more than ever before, for despite all the lofty knowledge of Doctors and Saints, there remain " great depths to be fathomed in Christ," and only by suffering can they be attained. The union of profoundest joy and intense suffering can be understood only by the Saints, for whom suffering itself becomes consolation and thus loses its sting ; for " the soul that of a truth desires wisdom first desires truly to enter farther into the thicket of the Cross, which is the road of life, which few enter." For even in this highest state of the Transforming Union she will always receive new light on the Divine mysteries, and this light comes by suffering, by which she is ever more conformed to the Son of God, whom she desires to love as much as she is loved by Him, so that at last " the soul loves God with the will of God, which is also her own will ; and thus she will love Him even as much as she is loved by God." Then she is truly transformed into the Blessed Trinity by whose life she henceforth lives. " And this is for the soul so high a glory, and so profound and sublime a delight, that it cannot be described by mortal tongue, nor can human understanding, as such, attain to any conception of it."

It would seem that, after this, no more can be said of the mystic life, that the rest belongs to the realm of the ineffable. But St. John of the Cross was sent into the world to instruct souls in the most profound secrets of the Divine Union, and so he gave to them one more work, even more sublime than the *Spiritual Canticle*. The *Living Flame of Love*, too, is a commentary on a poem, a very short one of four stanzas of the sacred murmurings of a lover held in the embrace of the " Living Flame of Love, that tenderly woundest my soul in its deepest centre." These stanzas, in his own words, " relate to things so interior and spiritual that words commonly fail to describe them," and " treat of a love which is even more complete and perfected within this same state of trans- formation" described in the last chapters of the *Spiritual Canticle*. So this work begins where the other left off ; namely with the soul already in the state of the Transforming Union, " abounding in delights, for it perceives that from its belly are flowing the rivers of living water which the Son of God said would flow from such souls." This flame of love is the Holy Ghost, living and burning within the soul and refreshing her with His own Divine life. And as the actions of the soul are, therefore, in a way, Divine, each one of them is now of greater value in the eyes of God than all those she did before she came to this state.

Here lies the explanation of the power of intercession that strikes us so forcibly in the lives of the Saints. Why is it that some persons' prayers seem always to be answered and others hardly ever ? Why could a touch of St. Bernard's or Bl. Anna Taigi's hands heal the sick, and a word of the Curé d'Ars convert sinners whom the most eloquent sermons had been unable to touch ? Discounting exceptional favours, in the normal way of Divine Providence the efficacy of a person's prayer grows proportionately with his charity, and therefore it easily comes to pass that a poor Irish peasant woman may convert a heretic on whom a learned doctor has spent his arguments in vain. And as in the Transforming Union charity has attained to the heights, the smallest deeds of such persons are more powerful in the realm of grace than the greatest exertions of those in an inferior degree of love. "In this state, therefore," says the Saint, " the soul can perform no acts but it is the Holy Spirit that moves it to perform them ; wherefore all its acts are Divine "—which, of course, does not mean that they cease to be human ; but they are both, performed by the Holy Ghost working in the soul by her free consent. For this reason the soul " speaks of the flame as living ; . . . because its effect is to make the soul live spiritually in God."

This " Playing of God," this " feast of the Holy Spirit, takes place in the substance of the soul, where neither the devil nor the world nor sense can enter," that is to say in that most intimate region where she is *capax Dei,* in the *scintilla,* as Master Eckhart calls it, where God and the soul are oned. This most intimate union is incomparably superior to the state usually called Mystic Union (St. Teresa's Fifth Mansion). In it Wisdom, the highest of the Gifts of the Holy Ghost, completely absorbs the soul and, as she is now perfectly purified, causes her ineffable delight. She becomes fully conscious of the power and glory of the life to come, and her life on earth appears to her but as a thin web preventing her from perfect fruition of God, hence she prays that it may be broken, so that she may enter into the joy of her Lord. " For the soul in this state knows very well that it is the habit of God to take away such souls before their time in order to give them good things and to remove them from evil things, perfecting them in a short time by means of that love." For the soul is now wholly aflame with the Divine fire that " consumes not the spirits wherein it burns . . . but rather delights them and deifies them," and which enlarges the soul, making her fit for " a boundless consummation in glory " by " a touch of the Divinity in the soul, without any form or figure whether formal or imaginary," which he calls a " delectable wound." Through this wound the soul becomes " altogether wounded and altogether healthy," for it is inflicted " by One Who cannot but heal," and the ardent spirit of the Saint bursts forth in descriptions of enraptured beauty at the thought of the Divine hand, " laid very firmly but very lovingly and graciously upon my soul."

It is hardly possible for anyone with a sense for the spiritual not to be carried away by these outpourings of a soul that has attained to the limits to which mystic experience in this life can reach. But if it is right that these descriptions should be read by beginners, frightened by the uncompromising austerity of the *Ascent* and the *Dark Night,* in order to show them the goal to which all the suffering and abnegation is to lead, it is also necessary to warn them against illusions. For in the face of the highest mystical experience human language is hopelessly inadequate ; it can be expressed only in metaphors and symbols. Now, in the beginning of the spiritual life God normally sends great sensible sweetness and feelings of delight, and when the inexperienced soul reads the *Spiritual Canticle* or the *Living Flame of Love* she may easily be led astray and think that the things described there are similar to her own experiences. A novice in mountaineering is frequently deceived in a similar way. Having climbed a little it seems to him that he can almost touch the top of the mountain with his hand. If he acted on this impression and sat down to have a good rest, convinced that another half an hour's climb will bring him to the top, he would be sorely disappointed, and the night would overtake him before he was even half way to his goal. Thus the novice in the spiritual life, deceived by his sweet feelings, might imagine that he is quite near the region of the *Living Flame*, an illusion which would completely ruin his progress. As a matter of fact the *Living Flame*, as St. John of the Cross himself admits, describes states reserved only to the very few who have had the courage to go the way of annihilation of self right to the end and which are reached only after long years of the most painful purgations. By the overwhelming majority of readers, therefore, the work will most profitably be read as an enchanting description of a land which they can hardly hope to reach in this life, but the very knowledge of whose existence will spur them on to more generous effort and to the patient enduring of suffering and temptation. For, as the Saint repeats so often, " souls which attain to this lofty kingdom have commonly passed through many trials and tribulations . . ." for " delight and knowledge of God cannot well find a home in the soul if sense and spirit be not thoroughly purged and strengthened and purified." And this is precisely why so few souls arrive at this sublime union. " Not," as St. John insists, " because God is pleased that there should be few raised to this high spiritual state—on the contrary, it would please Him if all were so raised—but rather because He finds few vessels in whom He can perform so high and lofty a work."

It is only by dying to all the natural movements and operations of the soul that she can attain to the true life in which " the substance of the soul, although it is not the Substance of God, for into this it cannot be changed, is nevertheless united in Him and absorbed

in Him, and is thus God by participation in God, which comes to
pass in this perfect state of the spiritual life, although not so perfectly as in the next life." Then "the soul with its faculties is
illumined within the splendours of God" and wholly moved and
enkindled by the Holy Ghost, and memory, understanding and
will, which in the Dark Night were empty, are now filled to overflowing with God. "For in this state the soul truly sees that God
belongs to it, and that it possesses Him with hereditary possession,
as an adopted child of God, by rightful ownership," and therefore
can give God to Himself, as He has given Himself to her. This
reciprocal love is the Mystic Marriage, "wherein the possessions
of both, which are the Divine Essence, are possessed likewise by
both together in the voluntary surrender of each to the other."
For the soul now loves God not through herself, but through God,
"since it loves through the Holy Spirit, even as the Father loves the
Son." At this stage all created beauty that the soul had to renounce in order to attain to Divine Union is given back to her
transfigured, for now she no longer sees God in creatures, but
creatures in God, and "they also reveal the beauties of their being,
virtue, loveliness and graces . . . and there is revealed to it (the soul)
in this great renewal that Divine life and the being and harmony
of every creature in it which has its movements in God. . ." All
is at last consummated. The soul has perfect fruition of God, and
with Him of all creation. Love has found its utter fulfilment, to
be surpassed only in the Beatific Vision of Heaven. "At eventide,
they will examine thee in Love"—in the first and greatest Commandment, of which the mystic life is but the perfect fulfilment.

CONCLUSION

THE GREAT REALITIES : PRAYER AND PENANCE

WHEN we consider the lives of the mystics not from the theological point of view as circles whose centre is God, but rather from the psychological angle, they present themselves as ellipses, as it were, with the two focal points of prayer and penance. As such, for all the present day interest in mysticism, they seem rather remote from our time, which prefers action to contemplation and enjoyment of earthly goods to voluntary renunciation. Modern men and women desire to live " full lives," by which they mean a participation as far as possible in all kinds of activities and enjoyments, whether politics or sports, science or the arts, social events or private " romances." They desire them all, and wireless, film and news-papers compete to give them an increasingly large share in them. Thus, to the inevitable material noise of modern life there is added a kind of constant spiritual noise in men's minds and hearts, the perpetual taking in of new things one after the other, which are never assimilated, and the equally perpetual craving for more. When this incessant flow stops, for instance through illness, there is a great emptiness, for the poor soul has nothing to fall back on—she is a " pipe," as St. Bernard calls it, through which flow many things, but which retains nothing.

This is the unhappy state of modern men and women without number, who live in a vicious circle. They begin by filling up their existence—or by having it filled up for them by others—with so much interior and exterior noise that the " still small voice " of God and of their own conscience is smothered. Then comes a moment—as it will come even in the most crowded life —when the noise stops and the soul is left alone with herself. But by this time she has become all but deaf to the Voice, and in her horror of the void she plunges into another round of ceaseless activity—and so it goes on. For if the Voice of God is to be heard in the soul two things are necessary : she must open her ears, which is done by prayer, and she must silence those voices that would interfere with the Divine Voice, which is done by penance. There is a kind of devils, as Our Lord told His desciples, that cannot be driven out save by prayer and fasting. Who, after the revelations of Lourdes and Fatima, can imagine that the devils of our time can be exorcised by any other means ?

For prayer and penance are the two mainsprings of the spiritual life, and if we would know what man can accomplish by them we must ask the mystics : The blind see and the lame walk, the lepers are cleansed and the deaf hear, the dead are raised and the poor have the Gospel preached to them. These are now as 1900 years ago the signs that proclaim the Christ-Life—but the Christ-Life means the crucified life. We men of the twentieth century are used to shortcuts : we lift the receiver and dial a number—and there is the voice of a friend at the other end. We cannot do this with God. In a way, though, to make contact with Him is even easier : we need only turn our will towards Him and it is established. But once we have lifted this receiver of our will we are not allowed to lay it down again. It must remain constantly in attendance on God, whether we hear His Voice or whether there is silence " at the other end " ; and neither material advantage nor fear, neither boredom nor depressions—*acedia* as the monks of old used to call it—are henceforth permitted to turn the will away from God. For prayer is the work of a lifetime. It is, indeed, a *work*. It begins with " saying our prayers," with making a short meditation every day—and it ends, if allowed to develop without hindrance, by absorbing and penetrating the whole man, so that his entire life is transformed into prayer. The secret of the amazing activity of so many mystics—we need only remember St. Bernard, St. Catherine, St. Teresa—is their life of prayer. And how could it be otherwise, as they are in such close union with Him who is *Actus Purus*, pure act ? But, unlike the great historical personages of this world, their action is always primarily directed to the advancement of the Kingdom of God and the salvation of souls ; their chief significance is on the spiritual, not on the material plane. St. Bernard was not a politician, nor St. Teresa a business-woman, though their particular vocations involved them in a bit of either. They were first and foremost lovers of God and of prayer. It is to prayer that our world must turn again if it would be saved from the evils that have befallen it ; and not to prayer only, but also to the salt of prayer, which is penance.

If prayer is rather unpopular to-day, penance is even more so.

People, even religious people, seem to have a veritable horror of
it. They fear not only that it might injure one's health, but hold
it to be bad even for the spiritual life, leading to pride and sin-
gularity. This attitude goes together with the secularism from
which our world is suffering. For nineteen centuries, ever since
St. Paul wrote that he was buffeting his body in order to bring it
into subjection, Christians have practised voluntary penances and
the Church has encouraged them. It would be strange, indeed,
if they should suddenly have become bad for the soul in the twentieth. It is true that, generally speaking, the nervous strain of
modern life makes certain physical austerities inadvisable for many ;
but even to-day hard-worked religious take the discipline and
wear hair shirts or sleep on planks and find themselves none the
worse for it. It is by no means those who treat their " Brother
Ass " most severely who suffer most from ill-health—God does
not normally punish souls for their generosity. On the contrary,
St. Teresa's experience that illness beats a retreat before penance
may frequently be repeated even to-day.

Nor is the other objection, namely that physical austerities
may lead to pride, of greater weight. It is a sad fact that, fallen
human nature being what it is, any activity may lead to this. If
it makes a man proud that he takes the discipline or has bread and
water for his breakfast, he will probably find equal food for
pride in attending daily Mass, in giving alms, or in any other
spiritual activity meant to lead to perfection. The great remedy
for all such temptations to take pride in the things that are done for
God is to look at the Crucifix and to consider what He has done
for us—then the greatest things a man can do or suffer will appear
as nothing, and, instead of being puffed up by her penitential
exercises, a soul will be ashamed that she can do only so little to
come nearer to God.

For the chief cause of our ills, of wars and famine, of materialism
and cruelty, is the terrifying estrangement from Him. Even the
most primitive savages have a piece of wood in which they believe
a Divine power to reside and which they adore—but many modern
Europeans have not even that. In the centre of their soul, which
is meant to be the dwelling-place of God, there is a void—a void
that cries out to be filled, and that is given stones for the Bread
of Life. It is, indeed, a sound instinct that makes so many of our
contemporaries turn to the mystics ; but if this new interest in

them is to bear the fruit that is so badly needed, they must be seen
not as interesting specimens of religious psychology but as men
and women set before us as our example. The forms that their
mystic experience takes are truly of amazing variety, but the foundation is always the same : it is the life of Grace springing up in the
soul at Baptism, and nourished by the other Sacraments of the
Church and by the soul's own activity in prayer and penance.
Thus the spiritual life is perfected in an interplay of public and
private worship. In the liturgy and the Sacraments the soul
confesses Christ before men ; in the hiddenness of her private
penances she fulfils Our Lord's command to enter into her inner
chamber and close the door against all but Him, who sees in secret.

For this is another characteristic of the mystic life too little
appreciated in our day : the highest union with God is achieved
only in solitude, though this solitude may sometimes have to be
only interior, as in the case of those mystics whose vocation is in
the world, and who rely on what St. Catherine calls the " inner
cell." " I will lead her into the desert and there I will speak to her
heart," says the Lord through Osee, for only in the desert can the
small still Voice make itself heard. But we love to do things in
crowds and teams—yet prayer and penance defy crowds. To do
penance in public, as the Flagellants did in the Middle Ages, only
leads to a religious exhibitionism that defeats the very object of
the penitential life which is to lead to perfect self-abnegation.
We may not be tempted to walk through the streets scourging
ourselves, but we may perhaps be inclined to abstain conspic-
uously from eating cake at a tea party in Lent, or to impose a not
very difficult rule of silence on ourselves when it would be more
charitable to speak. All such singularities fall under Our
Lord's condemnation of the hypocrites who like to appear to men
to fast. There are plenty of hidden penances and small sacrifices—
which to find out Ste. Thérèse de Lisieux was so ingenious—which
are much harder and can be done in perfect secrecy—it is these
that Our Lord teaches us to prefer, for they are the only ones acceptable to the Father. It is this hidden life of prayer and penance,
the life lived away from the limelight, unless it be placed before
men by a special Providence, that is most needed if the world is
to find its way back to the faith and charity that brings true peace.
It is a hard life, indeed, but it bears a wonderful promise. In the
Marriage Service of the Church bridegroom and bride promise

that they will take each other as husband and wife " for better or for worse . . . . till death do us part." The soul, too, is called to a marriage, to the marriage with her heavenly Spouse. She, too, must take her Divine Lord " for better or for worse "— but at the end of this spiritual marriage there is no sorrowful parting, but the ultimate fulfilment. For the bride-soul that takes the Lord for her spouse will make her vows to Him not " till death do us part," not until the bitter day of separation, but until the glorious day of perfect consummation, till, after long years of prayer and penance, of joy and suffering, " death do us unite."

BIBLIOGRAPHY

INTRODUCTION

R. Garrigou-Lagrange, O.P., *Christian Perfection and Contemplation according to St. Thomas Aquinas and St. John of the Cross.* Eng. trans. M. T. Doyle, 1937.
R. Garrigou-Lagrange, O.P., *The Three Ways of the Spiritual Life.* Eng. trans., 1938.
A. Poulain, S.J., *The Graces of Interior Prayer.* Eng. trans., L. L. Yorke Smith, 1910.
A. Saudreau, *The Mystical State.* Eng. trans., 1924.
A. Saudreau, *The Life of Union with God.* Eng. trans., 1927.
St. Thomas Aquinas, *Summa Theologica*, esp. Prima Secundæ Qu. LXVII and Secunda Secundæ Qu. XLV and QQ. CLXXIX–CLXXXII.

CHAPTER I

St. Bernard

Works in J. P. Migne, *PL.* 182–84.
Eng. trans. of *Sermons on the Canticle* by S. J. Eales, 1896, of *On the Love of God* by T. L. Connolly, 1937 ; and of *The Twelve Degrees of Humility and Pride* by B. R. V. Mills, 1929.
E. Vacandard, *Vie de St. Bernard*, 2 vols. (new ed. 1927).
A. J. Luddy, *Life and Teaching of St. Bernard* (Dublin, 1927).
W. W. Williams, *Studies in St. Bernard of Clairvaux* (1927).
E. Gilson, *The Mystical Theology of St. Bernard* (Eng. trans. 1940).

St. Hildegard

Works in Migne, *PL* 197.
F. M. Steele, *The Life and Visions of S. Hildegarde* (1915).

St. Catherine of Siena

The Dialogue, trans. A. Thorold, new ed., 1925.
A. T. Drane, *The History of St. Catherine of Siena and her Companions* (still the best Life in English).
A. Curtayne, *St. Catherine of Siena* (1929).

Bl. Anna Maria Taigi

R. F. Calixte, *Life of the Ven. Anna Maria Taigi.* Eng. trans., 1873.
K. Henvey, *A Mystic in the Home* (CTS, 1935).

CHAPTER II

H. de Hornstein, *Les grands mystiques allemands du XIVe siècle* (Luzerne, 1922)]

CHAPTER III

St. Bonaventure

Works, Quarracchi edition, 1882–1902, especially vols. 5 and 8.
E. Gilson, *The Philosophy of St. Bonaventure.* Eng. trans. London, 1938.
E. Longpré, O.F.M., Article "Bonaventure" *in Dictionnaire de Spiritualité.*

Bl. Angela de Folign

Le Livre de la Bienheureuse Angele de Foligno, ed. P. Doncoeur, S.J., 1926.

LOUISE LATEAU,

M. Didry and A. Wallemacq, *Louise Lateau of Bois-d'Haine*, Eng. trans. Dom Fran
Izard, O.S.B.

Dr. Paul van Gehuchten, *Etude médicale des Stigmat es de Louise Lateau*, in *Etude
Carmélitaines*, No. 20, vol. 2, Oct. 1936.

CHAPTER IV

ST. GERTRUDE

Works, ed. by the Benedictines of Solesmes (1875).
Dom Gilbert Dolan, *St. Gertrude the Great* (1912).

ST. MARGARET MARY

A. Hamon, S.J., *Vie de Sainte Marguerite-Marie* (l. ed., 1907).
H. Ghéon, *The Secret of St. Margaret Mary* (tr. 1937).

CHAPTER V

ST. TERESA

Eng. trans. of her *Works* by E. Allison-Peers.
H. H. Colville, *St. Teresa of Spain*.
J. J. Burke, *St. Teresa of Jesus*.
R. Hoornaert, *St. Teresa in her Writings* (Eng. trans., 1931).
E. Allison-Peers, *Mother of Carmel* (1945).

ST. FRANCIS DE SALES

Introduction to the Devout Life, new Eng. ed., 1937, trans by A. Ross.
Treatise on the Love of God, abridged trans., 1931.
E. J. Sanders, *St. François de Sales* (1928).
H. C. Bordeaux, *St. Francis de Sales*. Eng. trans., 1929.
A. Saudreau, *Mystic Prayer according to St. Francis de Sales*. Eng. trans. A. E. H.
Swinstead, 1929.

CHAPTER VI

Works of St. John of the Cross, trans. by E. Allison Peers.
P. Bruno de Jésus-Marie, *Saint Jean de la Croix*.
P. Bruno de Jésus-Maric, *Vie D'Amour de Saint Jean de la Croix*.
J. Baruzi, *Saint Jean de la Croix et le problème de l'expérience mystique* (1931).
E. Allison Peers, *Spirit of Flame* (1943).